What People Are Saying About
Loving Without Spoiling

"Laden with practical advice for everyday parental challenges."
—Karen MacPherson, *Pittsburgh Post-Gazette*

"Highly focused chapters that are perfect for browsing or choosing topics of particular interest. Clear, direct, and nonrepetitive. The message is grounded in common sense and is remarkably consistent. Engaging from cover to cover."
—Mark Kolakowski, *Big Apple Parent*

"A great book for any parent—full of reminders and strategies that will help keep you on the right track when it comes to parenting your children with a balance between firm discipline and healthy doses of love and humor."
—Kevin MacKinnon, *City Parent*

"Our company, BookSmart, cannot keep Nancy Samalin's book *Loving Without Spoiling* in stock. The response has simply been overwhelming. Parents and teachers have been thrilled with Samalin's practical, straightforward approach to communicating with children. This book is fantastic and a must for parents and teachers!"
—Nancy Solomon, owner, BookSmart

"*Loving Without Spoiling* is a pleasure to read. The format makes it easy to find any topic quickly. The book confirms what you are doing right and offers great suggestions for those times when things aren't going quite the way you would like. I thoroughly enjoyed the humor in Nancy's writing and her willingness to share her child-rearing experiences. Great book for every parent and grandparent. Awesome!"
—Doris Patterson, child-care director and consultant

"*Loving Without Spoiling* is flat out the best book I have read on how to help parents! I can tell that Nancy has 'been in the trenches.' Her practical, down-to-earth tips are written in such a lighthearted, loving way that it is impossible to not come away from reading this book both inspired and motivated."

—Jay Leon, Jay Leon Learning Programs

"This is the book I would like to hand all new parents as they begin their journey. Nancy Samalin has provided a map for parents to help them navigate the bumps and blind curves on the road to raising happy, responsible children. Experienced parents will recognize and appreciate the jewels of wisdom in this practical and wise guide."

—Maureen Murphy, director, The Children's School,
Stamford, Connecticut

"Simple, practical advice that helps parents understand the goals they have for their children and how to achieve them by parenting with appropriate boundaries. As the director of an early childhood program, I'm excited by the opportunity parents have when they implement the positive advice contained in this book."

—Janet Reinertsen, director, St. Anne's Day School,
Atlanta, Georgia

"In *Loving Without Spoiling*, Nancy Samalin is at her best, using examples from real families to show how specific words and actions can help parents bring out the best in their kids—and themselves. Good parenting requires more than instinct and common sense; it's a skill that we develop with help from practical and compassionate teachers like Nancy."

—Amy Bean, mother of two, Warba, Minnesota

"Invaluable in addressing parents' issues and questions in a concise and thoughtful format. The quick reference guide is brilliant and each chapter a gem."

—Julia Randall, working mother

loving
without
spoiling

And 100 Other Timeless Tips

for Raising Terrific Kids

Nancy Samalin

with Catherine Whitney

Contemporary Books

Chicago   New York   San Francisco   Lisbon   London   Madrid   Mexico City
Milan   New Delhi   San Juan   Seoul   Singapore   Sydney   Toronto

Library of Congress Cataloging-in-Publication Data

Samalin, Nancy.
    Loving without spoiling : and 100 other timeless tips for raising terrific kids /
Nancy Samalin with Catherine Whitney.
        p.   cm.
    Includes index.
    ISBN 0-8092-9551-2 (hardcover) — ISBN 0-07-142492-X (paperback)
    1. Child rearing.   2. Parenting.   3. Parent and child.   I. Whitney,
Catherine.   II. Title.

HQ769.S2554   2003
649'.1—dc21   2002067513

1 2 3 4 5 6 7 8 9 0   AGM/AGM   2 1 0 9 8 7 6 5 4 3

ISBN 0-8092-9551-2 (hardcover)
ISBN 0-07-142492-X (paperback)

This book is printed on acid-free paper.

IN MEMORY of those who perished on September 11, 2001, whose deaths remind us to hold our families close and to cherish each precious day with them.

Contents

Part 3 ▪ Lend Support Without Hovering

Part 4 ▪ Show Love Without Spoiling

Part 5 ▪ Open Communication Channels

Part 6 ▪ Use Positive Discipline

Part 7 ▪ Develop Sibling Harmony

Part 8 ▪ Teach Social Skills

Part 9 ▪ Build Self-Esteem

Part 10 ■ Strengthen Parenting Skills

Acknowledgments

To Judith McCarthy, my editor, for her belief in and support of my work, her unremitting enthusiasm, her consistent good humor, and her valuable insights.

To Catherine, the collaborator for my last three books, who was tireless in helping to clearly articulate my ideas and organize my thoughts. I appreciate the grace, endless patience, and true professionalism of her work.

To Jane Dystel, the kind of agent any author would give her eyeteeth for. She has been an enthusiastic source of support during the publication of my last three books and, although she is one of the busiest people I know, always responds promptly to every request. I also appreciate the cooperation and responsiveness of her colleagues Miriam Goderich and Jo Fagan.

To Lizz Aviles, my publicist at McGraw-Hill, who is a treasure. I am grateful for her willingness to go beyond the call of duty, and I hope we'll be working together for a long time.

To Cory Zacker, whose calm and objective input into this book has been very helpful. And to Janet Schuler, for her skill in organizing and assisting in the research and preparation of material.

To the thousands of parents who have attended my workshops and speeches. You have been a constant source of inspiration and information and have taught me so much. I wish I could thank each of you individually because, without you, this book would not have been possible. Many of the examples, dialogues, and suggestions in this book are a result of your participation in my ongoing workshops and have kept me in touch with what parents are going through on a day-to-day basis.

I have been blessed with many special friends and colleagues whose encouragement and support have meant so much. My heartfelt appreciation goes to Margie Abrams, the late and much-loved Joe Anderson, Dr. Shelley Anderson, Judy Baker, Dr. Larry Balter, Cindy Beckler, Arlette Brauer, Linda Braun, Dr. Robert Brooks, Ann Caron, Jacqui Caruso-Smith, Barbara Coloroso, Elizabeth Crow, Debbie Dermer, Michael Eanes, Marty Edelston, Cheryl Flood, Alice Freedman, Arlynn Greenbaum, Barbara Hemphill, Ruth Hersh, Bel Kaufman, Andrea Kiernan, Lisa de Kooning, Dr. Lawrence Kutner, Nancy Kelem Landau, Vicki Lansky, Susan Lapinski, Esther and Mike Levine, Georgette McBreen, Florence Mitchell, Hal Morgan, Ann Pleshette Murphy, Doris Patterson, Dr. Alvin Rosenfeld, Dr. Bobbie Rowland, Marvin Terban, Len and Marilyn Weinstock, and Ira Wolfman.

I am also blessed with an exceptional family: my sister and brother-in-law, Ellen and Tom, who are always there for me; my late brother, Tom, who will be forever missed; and my mother, whose chronological age of ninety has done nothing to diminish her sharp wit, irreverence, high energy, and joy for life.

And to my sons, Eric and Todd, who are compassionate, trustworthy, loving men of whom I am immensely proud. They've forgiven me for my early parenting mistakes, and I treasure the love, openness, trust, and laughter in our relationship. What's more, they still groan affectionately at my corny jokes.

Finally, to Sy, my beloved husband, who has given me the gift of unending love, respect, true friendship, laughter, joy, and devotion.

Introduction

Parenting Skills for the New World

For the past twenty-five years, I've had the privilege of working with and speaking to thousands of caring, committed parents of toddlers through teens. The vast majority of them approach the task of raising children with love and optimism. Most hope that love will see them through but don't know what to do when love alone isn't enough. They are looking quite simply for specific guidelines that will enable their best sides—and their children's best sides—to shine through.

I've written this book to serve as a daily guide to skillful parenting. Each of the 100 topics focuses on an actual situation that typically occurs in families. For each situation, I tell you what you can do *right now* to resolve the conflict—including the words and actions that have made a difference in countless families.

Parenting seems to be the only job in which we tend to do the same things over and over again—even though they're not working. Maybe it's because we have the false hope that if only we repeat them enough, our children will eventually change their behavior for the better! It makes no sense, but I understand the tendency, having done the same thing myself when my kids were young. For example, I was guilty of being an endless nagger and incessant order giver. It didn't work at all. My sons just became "mother-deaf" and tuned me out. You'd think I would've given it up and tried different, more effective, strategies. Unfortunately, I was stuck in the rut of the familiar. But if something isn't working, as loving parents we all have the choice of changing our approach by trying new and better ways to communicate with our kids.

We hear today that kids are more spoiled than ever before. Parents are constantly being accused of "letting their kids get away with murder," allowing them to be rude and disrespectful, overindulging them, rescuing them instead of allowing them to experience consequences. The list is endless. People are quick to blame parents for all their children's mistakes. Instead of offering solutions, relatives deliver criticism, bystanders tut-tut—and that's not to mention single friends who are convinced they'd do a lot better if they had kids of their own.

In *Loving Without Spoiling*, instead of blaming parents and overloading them with "shoulds" or dire predictions of what will happen if they give in to their kids, I do just the opposite. This book offers practical guidelines, tips, examples, and dialogues that will help parents feel less guilty about setting limits and more competent and confident in their interactions with their children.

As I explain in this book in more detail, we're not doing children any favors by granting their every wish. Their wants are a bottomless pit and have to be limited. Since children themselves do not know the difference between their wants and needs, it's our job as loving parents to make the distinction.

Look carefully at your day, from the moment you wake up (or your kids waken you) until your kids are in bed (let's hope to stay), and allow yourself to take advantage of the many strategies that countless parents have so generously shared with me. The best of these ideas are incorporated into this book in an easily accessible format that even the busiest parent can use.It is my fervent wish that as you begin to learn and apply these skills, you—like many others over the years—will find a sense of empowerment, a confidence that holds steady even during the toughest times, and above all, a daily experience of the joy of being a parent.

Loving
Without Spoiling

PART 1

■

Avoid Power Struggles

1. Set Rules That Stick

Your responsibility as a parent is to set appropriate limits, keep your child healthy and safe, and establish order in your home. But you can find a balance between firmness and flexibility. In every family, there are both negotiable and nonnegotiable issues. When you examine the behavior issues in your household, you'll find that each of them fits into one of these two categories. The *nonnegotiable rules* relate to safety, health basics, and fundamental values. *Negotiable rules* are those you can bend, even if the behavior annoys you. They involve personal preferences, differing tastes, and convenience.

If you look at most rules, you can find several different ways of achieving the desired end. When you give your child the option of deciding how the goal is to be reached and allow her to feel more in control, she'll be less likely to resist. If the rule is that she must bathe daily, but she fights and stalls all the way into the tub, give her the option of substituting showers or the occasional sponge bath. If she balks at wearing a heavy jacket on a chilly day and insists she doesn't need it, let her take it along in a shopping bag to put on when she feels cold. If she always complains that she's not tired at bedtime, tell her she can keep the light on and read quietly as long as she stays in her bed. When she's tired enough, she'll fall asleep.

When you provide your child with some freedom and flexibility in everyday matters, you'll discover that she responds well

■ Be Clear, Firm, and Nonconfrontational

Don't say: "Why isn't your seat belt on?"
Instead, say: "When you've buckled up, we'll go."

Don't say: "You've got a fresh mouth."
Instead, say: "I won't listen when you speak to me rudely."

Don't say: "How many times have I told you to get ready for school?"
Instead, say: "The bus leaves in five minutes, and I expect you to be ready for it."

Don't say: "If you don't put those dishes in the dishwasher right now, you can't play with the computer tonight."
Instead, say: "You can use the computer as soon as these dishes are cleared away."

to the challenge of making her own decisions and sees that life usually offers a number of alternative possibilities.

Your tone of voice and the words you use can make all the difference between an angry power struggle and a spirit of reciprocity. The key is to state your rules and expectations clearly and firmly. Avoid showing anger when you state expectations. A display of anger only increases your child's resistance to your message.

I often suggest to parents that they make separate lists of nonnegotiable and negotiable issues. Keep in mind that "negotiable" doesn't mean anything goes, just that flexibility is possible. Here are some examples:

Negotiable Rules
What clothing to wear
When the lights go out
TV time limits and program selection
Food preferences
Choice of chores

Nonnegotiable Rules
No crossing the street without a parent or a responsible adult
    present
No insults or put-downs
No hurting or hitting
Clean up your own mess
Brush your teeth before bed
Complete homework before watching TV
Always wear a seat belt in the car
No cursing or bathroom language

This approach requires effort and patience, especially in the beginning. When you're tired or busy, or when your child is being particularly adamant, it may feel impossible. It's so tempting to give in to avoid a scene or argument. But in the long run, getting your kids to take your nonnegotiable rules seriously will not only reduce your stress, it will also teach them an important lesson in self-discipline.

2. Tame the Tantrums

Sometimes it can seem as if tantrums are a toddler's primary means of communication. The piercing screams and the flood of tears can signal tiredness, frustration, hunger, anger, disappointment, or discomfort. Tantrums can drive parents crazy and make *them* feel like wailing and flailing about, too.

As unpleasant as they are, tantrums are perfectly normal for young children—and they aren't a matter of behaving or not behaving. A small child literally can't repress his feelings. He lives in a melodramatic universe, where every matter is of extreme importance. He also lacks the language skills to express his feel-

---

■ **Parent's Story: Dad's Tantrum Tamer (don't try this in public . . .)**
A dad in one of my workshops described his response to three-year-old
Charlie's tantrums: "I'd lie down on the floor, kick my legs, and wave my
arms wildly until Charlie's screaming tantrum turned into an insane fit of
giggles."

---

ings. And depending on how you respond to tantrums, he may
learn that throwing himself on the floor, kicking his feet, and
screeching is the best way to get what he wants.

What can you do when your toddler is in the throes of a tantrum? Here are some practical suggestions:

- **Offer a distraction.** Young children have very short attention spans. Try diverting her with a toy, song, or change of
  scene.
- **Provide help.** Sometimes a child will have a tantrum
  because he's frustrated. Ease the frustration by quietly helping him put on his shoes or showing him how a toy works.
- **Plan ahead.** Some tantrums can be avoided by being in
  tune with a child's internal clock. Try to maintain a regular
  schedule for meals and naps. If you have to be out of the
  house, be sure to take along a snack. Try to plan excursions
  for times when your toddler is well fed and rested.
- **Be firm but calm.** If your child's tantrum triggers an
  angry, loud response from you, it's likely to escalate. Keep
  your voice low, and offer comfort if needed. For example,
  instead of shouting, silently take your child in your arms
  and hug her.
- **Don't give in once you've said no.** If tantrums occur
  because your child wants something that you don't want to
  give him, don't let yourself be manipulated. In the long
  run, giving in to tantrums only inspires more tantrums.

For example: A friend's two-year-old son had terrible temper tantrums when he didn't get what he wanted. His ear-piercing shrieks were so terrible that his mother found it was often easier to cave in to his demands rather than to put up with another episode. This little boy is now almost four, and his tantrums have become an automatic reaction when he doesn't get his way.

Unfortunately, when we give in to demands after saying no, we're setting ourselves up for the behavior to be repeated. Children learn that throwing tantrums, whining, screaming, or hitting is effective. It's only natural, then, that children apply what they learn and use the same techniques over and over again.

It's better to wait out the tantrum or, if your child doesn't stop, remove him from the scene. Get down to his eye level and say, quietly but firmly, "I know you really want me to buy you that candy, but we're only getting groceries today."

Try to remember, too, that tantrums don't last forever. By the time your child has a command of the language and can tell you in words what she wants and how she feels, she won't need to express herself by wailing.

3. Survive the Public Meltdown

Every trip we take with our kids into the outside world is potentially full of pitfalls. We can't predict what will happen, and we seldom feel competent when our kids embarrass us in front of other people. Few things are harder for a parent to endure than a child who is imposing her disruptive behavior on innocent bystanders: the child who has a tantrum on a crowded bus, the shrieking baby surrounded by business travelers on an airplane shuttle, the restless toddler in a long line, the obstinate child who won't budge from the middle of the floor in a busy waiting room, the child with a high-decibel voice making so much noise in a restaurant that you can almost hear the stomachs churning around you.

It's always uncomfortable when your child is the source of aggravation to others. You know people are annoyed, and you feel so helpless.

Often other adults don't appreciate the fact that young children who are tired, hungry, or bored haven't learned to sit on those feelings. Even when they sympathize with the kids, they still may be annoyed when parents don't intervene effectively. In many of these situations, bystanders may feel just as restless and

---

■ Tips: Ease the Stress of Flying with a Toddler

- Plan for your trip. A five-hour airplane flight is bound to be too confining for the average toddler and very stressful for you. Prepare diversions—games, toys, books, drawing paper, drinks, and snacks. Be prepared to give her a lot of attention. Don't forget to bring a favorite lovey or blanket.
- Feed her on takeoff and descent, the two times when she must be restrained. A bottle, cup, or pacifier can comfort her. Babies and young children often cry and get distressed because of pain in their ears, especially upon descent. Sucking or swallowing will relieve the pressure.
- Request an aisle seat so that you can take her for a walk up and down the aisle every half hour or so. This is especially crucial for a very active child.
- Try not to feel too bad. Although you know that the adults around you might not enjoy the company of a squirmy, fussy child, that's just the way it is. Children are an integral part of public life, and your child is merely behaving normally for her age.

---

irritated as the children. Kids merely act out openly what everyone else is experiencing because they haven't yet acquired the ability for self-restraint.

Kids Will Be Kids

Ever wonder why your child seems to save his tantrums for when you're in public? Well, the next time your three-year-old throws herself on the floor, kicking and screaming, or your seven-year-old decides it's cool to use a curse word in the middle of the mall, stop and ask yourself a different question: If you *weren't* out in public, would you be as upset? I'm not condoning rude or unruly behavior. However, many parents have a tendency to overreact when disapproving strangers are around.

When kids act up at home, whether it's a temper tantrum or a fresh mouth, parents can usually handle it more calmly. However, there's an unspoken expectation by many people that children should act like little adults in public. And the opinion of critical bystanders can take on more importance than it should. We feel like we're on display, being reprimanded by a critical and unsympathetic audience.

Unfortunately, the myth of the well-behaved child is pervasive, especially with adults who are not parents themselves. Onlookers, especially those without kids, are the most unforgiving, convinced that if they were the parent, *their* kids would never behave that way. Sometimes older people whose own children are grown have forgotten what kids are like. I've had grandparents complain heartily about restless toddlers, making statements like, "He never sits still!" or, "She makes so much noise!" or even, "These days, parents let their kids get away with murder."

It's easy to buy into the guilt that others try to impose on you, the frazzled parent. You don't want your child to be a problem any more than they do. But unlike the people around you, you have the primary responsibility for the comfort and well-being of your child. Sometimes the only thing you can do is silently repeat the mantra "I don't know these people. I'll never see them again. They are not my friends."

■ **Parent's Story: See No Evil, Hear No Evil**

Cathy's son, Jonah, just shy of two years old, was screaming uncontrollably in his stroller while passersby made remarks such as, "Why can't she shut that kid up?" and "God, what a brat." Even though Jonah is her first child and it was hard, especially as a new parent, not to get defensive, Cathy realized that the uncivil behavior was coming not only from Jonah but from the commentators as well. She decided to let their remarks roll off her back, refusing to be judged by the rudeness of strangers.

---

4. Stop the Whining

You're sitting at the kitchen table, trying to write a card to a friend, when your six-year-old interrupts you. It's the third time in three minutes.

"I'm bored," he whines.

Without looking up, you say, "Stop whining. I told you I'd be finished soon."

His voice rises to a higher pitch. "But, Mommy, I don't have anything to do."

"Then find something. I need to finish this note." Now your voice is angry.

"But Mommeeee!" His tone has now escalated to a siren wail. "What should I doooo?"

You throw down your pen and turn sharply around. "Stop that whining already. What do you want *me* to do? You've got a room full of toys."

The broken record plays on and on: He whines; you react. He whines some more; you raise your voice. He whines; you give in—or give up. It's understandable, and incredibly frustrating. When your child starts whining, all you can think of is getting him to stop.

Whining is like chalk scratching on the blackboard. It's as irritating as the nonstop bleat of a car alarm or a dog barking. And it can drive the most even-tempered parent over the edge. But most of the time, ordering a child to stop whining is about as effective as ordering an infant to stop crying.

Role-Playing: An Anti-Whining Strategy

When a child has developed a whining habit, she is usually unable to stop by herself. Carol, a mother in one of my workshops, tried to teach her four-year-old, Hannah, to identify the difference between whining and asking, so Hannah could gain more control over the way she expressed herself. When Hannah started to whine, Carol said, "I only answer when you speak in your regular Hannah voice, not the whiny voice. Can you ask me in a way that makes me want to listen?" In time, Hannah learned how to ask for what she wanted without whining. When she occasionally slipped, Carol learned to say calmly, "Try again. I'll bet you can say that in your regular Hannah voice."

Another six-year-old girl was such a whiner that her mother had trouble telling the difference between these voices:

Jennifer: *(whining)* I'm starved. *Puhleeeeze* . . . I need a snack.

Mom: You may have a snack if you ask me in your regular voice.

Jennifer: *(whining)* This *is* my regular voice!

Mom: It is? Are you sure?

Jennifer: Yesss!

Mom: OK, you be the mom, and I'll be Jennifer. I'm going to ask you for a snack in my regular voice.

Jennifer: *(starting to giggle)* OK.

Mom: *(in an exaggerated whine)* Mommeee, I'm starving. *Puh-leeeeze* . . . I need a snack.

Jennifer: *(laughing)* That's not my regular voice!

Mom: What a relief. I was getting worried. Now let me hear your regular voice.

Jennifer complied. She also became more conscious of the way she sounded when she was whining. What's more, she and her mother were able to share a laugh because the exercise was conducted in a fun, nonjudgmental way. Of course, if you try role-playing, be careful that you do it playfully, never sarcastically. Your goal is to teach, not to make fun of your child. Also, if your child is truly hungry or overtired, she won't be able to take in your words or appreciate your humor.

■ Parent's Story: Language Lessons

Sheila and her five-year-old daughter, Emily, were riding the bus. Two rows away, a little boy was badgering his mother in a high-pitched, annoying whine: "Mommy, please, can we go to the zoo? . . . Please . . . Please." As his pleading grew more shrill, others on the bus frowned with aggravation. Sheila watched her daughter, who in silent fascination gazed at the boy. Sheila thought she'd found the perfect "teachable moment" until Emily leaned over and whispered loudly, "Mommy, that boy talks whine, too!"

Don't cave in. An experienced whiner knows how to wear a parent down with his unrelenting pleas. If you're tempted to give up just to stop the whining, separate yourself from the child. Say, "If you're in a whiny mood, that's OK, but I don't want to hear it. You need to go to your room. You can whine there until you are ready to stop. I'll be in the kitchen, so come out when you're through."

One parent I know swears by the following rather original strategy. When her daughter starts whining, she hands her a tape recorder and says, "Why don't you go in the family room and tape it for me? I'll try to listen when I have a chance." Inevitably, her daughter has forgotten all about her grievance by the time Mom is ready to listen to the tape.

■ **Six Quick Responses to Nip Whining in the Bud**

Be sure to use your *own* nonwhining voice when giving these responses.

1. "You may ask me one more time.
2. "I can't listen when you're whining."
3. "Try a different voice."
4. "Whining will not change my no into a yes."
5. "It's OK to whine, as long as you do it in your room."
6. "Ouch! My ears are starting to hurt."

---

5. Transform Defiance into Cooperation

When children assert themselves at home or in public, their frustrated parents often ask themselves, "Who is in charge here?"

However, it's not very effective to respond to challenges to your authority with phrases such as *I set the rules around here* or *Because I said so*. Such statements aren't convincing or persuasive, and kids know it.

I have found there are better ways to resolve parent-child conflicts without shouting, making yourself crazy, or engaging in a power trip.

Deliberate Disobedience

Parents believe that their job is to set the rules and their children's job is to follow those rules. But frequently parents encounter situations when their children deliberately disobey them.

Here's a typical scenario: Mom tells her son he may ride his bike with his friends but that she needs him home in one hour. When he arrives home two hours later, with no real apology or excuse, naturally she's upset because the house rules or limits have been ignored.

Instead of getting angry, this mom will get results by being firm and enforcing consequences. It's essential for her son to know that she's going to stick to the rules. If she makes a threat and then *doesn't* follow through, she loses all credibility. Therefore, Mom, without losing her temper, must remain firm: "I know how much fun it is to ride your bike, but since you didn't come in when you were supposed to, you'll have to lose the privilege of using your bike this week." This response also teaches her son that being allowed to ride his bike with his friends is a privilege, not a right, and that with privileges come responsibilities.

Who's the Boss?

When children become defiant, they often say to their parents, "You're not the boss over me!" This was one of my son Todd's

■ **Parent's Story: The Paradoxical Response**

One father used the following strategy to tease out cooperation from resistance.

Jon: I don't wanna brush my teeth!
Dad: Right. You're not old enough to brush your teeth all by yourself. I bet you don't even know how!

Dad's response worked for Jon because he was a child who loved a challenge, and he jumped at the chance to prove his father wrong!

favorite expressions. I admit I sometimes sank to his level—angrily replying, "Yes, I am!" It wasn't a very effective reaction. A more skillful response would have been, "Boy, Todd, I know you hate it when people boss you around, but the clothes still need to be put in the hamper, not left on the floor."

Many power struggles can be avoided if we reduce the number of requests and rules we impose on our children—and stick to the most important ones. When children feel as if their parents are constantly ordering them around or making too many rigid rules, it's not surprising that they become uncooperative. Parents might need to be more flexible about less important rules and make it clear which ones are not up for discussion.

Parents also need to examine the tone in which they make their requests. For example, "Why can't you remember to take your dishes to the sink?" is not really a question but a criticism and a challenge. It won't encourage cooperation, and it's demeaning as well. A better way to handle this type of forgetfulness would be to express a request, such as, "When you're finished eating, I would appreciate your putting your dishes in the sink."

■ **Parent's Story: At the End of the Day**

"Lucy was two and a half, and I was still asking her to tidy her mess. Lucy would say, 'No, I won't, *you* do it,' so I'd bend down and say, 'OK, I'll do it *with* you. After all, at the end of the day, we have to pick up our toys.'

"This went on well into Lucy's third year. Then one day, Lucy had a playmate over. What a lovely mess they made of Lucy's bedroom. Toys were scattered everywhere. When it was time for Lucy's friend to leave, something amazing happened. Lucy asked her friend to help put the toys away. 'No, I don't want to,' said her friend. So Lucy replied, 'That's OK. I'll do it with you. At the end of the day, we have to pick up our toys.'

"I firmly believe that once we realize that kids learn from what we do, not what we tell them to do, then our daily tasks are made smoother and easier."

6. Get Through to Parent-Deaf Kids

Are your kids parent-deaf? Do you find yourself raising your voice so that you can be heard? Screaming and yelling to make a point? Begging and pleading to elicit a response? Repeating yourself like a broken record? Do any of these tactics work? Probably not. The result is that your children still don't listen—and you're a bundle of nerves.

What can you do when you need to get a child's attention and he's in the parent-deaf mode? Here are some suggestions to improve the likelihood that your kids *will* actually listen to your requests:

• **When you have something to say to your child, make your physical presence felt.** Instead of calling out from across a room or down the hall, go to your child and look him in the eye when you speak. With a younger child, bend down and touch him while you're talking.

• **Tell your child what to *do* instead of what *not* to do.**

Ineffective: "Don't run."
Effective: "Walk when you cross the street."

Ineffective: "Don't get paint on the table."
Effective: "Keep your paint on the paper."

• **Be clear and specific.**

Ineffective: "Don't litter."
Effective: "That's garbage. It goes in the garbage can."

Ineffective: "Hurry up! Come on!"
Effective: "The school bus will be here in ten minutes."

• **Give your child information.** Describe the problem. Information helps him figure out what to do.

Ineffective: "Get that food off the floor!"
Effective: "Ants come in the house when food is left on the floor."

If you want your children to *exactly* follow your directions, you must spell out *exactly* what you want them to do. I frequently hear parents use such ineffective phrases as "Pay attention," "Be nice," "Snap out of it," "Watch out," "Grow up," and "Act your age." The bottom line is that kids *will* listen—as long as you have something clear and concrete to say.

■ **Parent's Story: Hello in There**

Jody's eight-year-old daughter, Kelly, was determinedly parent-deaf. She made it a point never to answer the first time Jody called, and usually it took three or four tries to get a response. Finally one day, Jody got so frustrated that she marched over to her daughter with a high-beam flashlight and pointed the beam at her daughter's ear.

"What are you doing?" Kelly asked.

"I'm checking your ears," Jody replied calmly. "You have so much trouble hearing me when I ask you to set the table or clean your room, I think you must have got something stuck in there."

Kelly laughed, "OK, Mom, you made your point."

7. Don't Be Sidetracked by *Whys*

When Barbara became a parent, she swore she'd never utter the words *because I said so*. Her own parents had frequently responded to her questions that way, and she'd always resented it. But that was before she had an inquisitive child of her own. Now, as she races to get everyone out of the house in the morning, Barbara faces endless questions from four-year-old Natalie: "Why do I have to go to school? Why do you have to go to work? Why can't we stay home today and play?"

The first morning Natalie asked "why?" Barbara took the time to explain patiently—even though they were running late. "I thought I could nip the problem in the bud by clearly pointing out the reasons to Natalie," she recalls. "I told her about all the kids in my class who were waiting for me to come and be their teacher. I reminded her about what fun she had at preschool and how much her friends would miss her if she weren't there. I told her we would spend lots of time together over the weekend.

"When I was finished with my long and convincing list, Natalie looked at me with tears in her eyes and said, 'But *why*, Mommy?'

"Now we go through this routine every morning, and *because I said so* is looking better and better."

Do Kids Really *Need* a Reason?

When kids repeatedly ask "why?" they don't always require a reason. Often, they just want to get you to change your mind. "Why?" is their way of expressing displeasure with a decision you've made. Or it can be a way to get your attention.

Parents, meanwhile, often believe that if they take the time to explain their reasons, their kids will more readily comply and they can avoid making their children unhappy. Not so! When you try to reason with your child about why he can't have a cookie, stay up late, or ride his bike in the dark, your goal is to get him to see things your way—to give up wanting what he wants. His goal is quite different: to nudge you from a no to a yes.

Children don't do this because they are naughty, obstinate, or deliberately indifferent to your explanations. Reasoning is an acquired skill, which requires a cognitive ability that young children don't yet possess. Before age three or four, children react to situations based on their emotions and their physical comfort levels. Between the ages of four and six, they gain a limited understanding of the way the world works but still lack well-developed reasoning skills. They live in the moment. When your young child wants to stay up past her bedtime and you say no, she won't be satisfied by your explanation that she'll be tired in the morning. She is totally engaged in the here and now, and isn't the least bit concerned with how she might feel the next day.

Trying to reason with a child who lacks the ability to be reasonable leads to frustration on both sides. Not only does the child remain unconvinced, but you may find that when your explanations don't work, you become angrier than if you hadn't offered any at all. The more time you invest, the greater your resentment: "Here I went to all this effort to explain, and she's still not satisfied!"

Answer a Question with Another Question

When kids ask serious questions that are truly a search for clarity, information, or understanding, they almost never start with "Why can't I?" or "Why won't you let me?" Serious questions do merit discussion or a thoughtful explanation. But most kids' "why" questions are designed simply to engage you—and rarely in a positive way. They *enjoy* trying to get you to change your mind. I call their talent for endless questioning and prodding "the sandpaper technique." They ask and ask and ask until all your resistance is worn away.

Any question that begins, "Why can't I?" or "Why won't you let me?" should send up a red flag—especially if you've answered it before. It's pointless to keep repeating the same explanation. Instead, turn the question around and put the onus on your child to answer it. One mom in my workshop has a child who comes up with a constant stream of curiosity whys, such as "Why do those people have a broken fence?" When she answers, he comes up with another why, then another. So she turns it into a thinking game, saying, "I'll think of one reason, then you think of another."

Turning the question around can be extremely effective, as another mother in my workshop discovered when she used it with her six-year-old son:

Tony: Why can't I have a gerbil?

Mom: We've been through this before.

Tony: But why can't I?

Mom: I'll bet you know the answer to that. You tell me.

Tony: *(reluctantly)* Because we already have a cat and a rabbit, and we don't have any more room?

Mom: Right. Those are all good reasons.

This approach is a gentle way of reminding your child that you've already been around this track numerous times and that you have faith in his ability to figure out the answer himself. It requires him—the person asking the question—to take the answer more seriously. This tactic lets you engage your child in a positive way and puts him in the position of reinforcing your message. What's more, he ends up feeling good because he has come up with his own answers.

Many parents tell me they want to learn from the mistakes their own parents made and do it differently. While they accept the fact that children need rules and guidelines, they are determined to find a warmer, more child-friendly style of parenting than they experienced in the authoritarian households of their

---

■ **You Know You're Sidetracked When . . .**
- After you've provided a full explanation, your child wails, "But *why?*"
- You find yourself saying, "As I've told you before . . ."
- The next word after *why* is *can't* or *not*, as in "Why can't I?" and "Why not?"
- You notice that the "why can't I?" questions usually come when you're rushed, busy, tired, or out in public.
- Your goal is to convince your child that you're right and she's wrong.
- You're so exhausted by explanations and counterarguments that you start wavering and just give in.

youth. In the process, they often discover ways to make their no seem less abrupt and "I'm the boss" sound more like "I'm in charge." And they learn the best lesson there is: *You can be loving and still say no!*

8. Be Authoritative

It's the job of parents to set limits. But it's the goal of children to try to wriggle out of them at every opportunity. We must provide structure; they want freedom. We need to ensure their safety; they are attracted to adventure and danger. We are aware of consequences; they are impulsive and fully immersed in the here and now.

We cannot force children to see things from our perspective. It's a tempting idea because it would make our lives so much easier. But just imagine your child saying, "You're right, Mommy. I shouldn't get to watch TV until I finish my homework. Thank you so much for reminding me." It's an absurd image. Even so, many parents desperately try to coax their children into happy compliance. Or they go to the other extreme, putting on their "law enforcement" hats and becoming rigid and controlling.

Fortunately, the choice does not have to be between being too permissive or too strict. There's another way—it's called being authoritative. Let's look at the three styles: too permissive, too strict, and authoritative.

Too Permissive

Being permissive means bribing and pleading and often giving in. It means needing your child to be happy with the limits you impose. It means saying no but meaning "probably not" or "I'm not sure." It's like the parent who told me, "We've set very clear rules around bedtime . . . I *think*."

Permissiveness may feel loving in the moment, but it breeds insecurity. A child can't handle having too much power. No matter how much he protests or argues, he needs you to be in charge—in a loving way.

Here's a typical scenario that demonstrates permissive parenting in action. Kevin, age six, is allowed to play in the backyard after supper. At eight o'clock, Mom calls him to come in:

> **Mom:** Kevin, darling, it's getting dark out. How about coming in?
> **Kevin:** No, I don't want to.
> **Mom:** Please, dear.
> **Kevin:** No. I want to play outside for half an hour more.
> **Mom:** It's getting late. Be good and come in, OKaaay . . . ?
> **Kevin:** No!

Kevin runs off into the yard while Mom complains, "I can't do anything with that child." But by allowing Kevin to set the terms, Mom has lost the battle. Given a choice, kids will rarely pick the option that isn't fun.

Recently I observed an example of a parent asking a child for permission. I watched a dad having a snack at a coffee shop with his daughter, who looked to be about three years old. He hadn't finished, but he noticed her getting a bit restless. I overheard him say, "Is it OK with you if I finish my coffee before we go?" I was struck by his desire to let her take charge. Had he been more authoritative, he could've said something like, "As soon as I finish my coffee, we'll leave."

▨ What's Your Parenting Style?

SITUATION	TOO PERMISSIVE	TOO STRICT	SIMPLY AUTHORITATIVE
Your preschooler cries for candy at the super-market.	"Oh, all right. I'm too tired to argue. But just this once."	"I told you no, and I mean no! If you ask me again, there will be no candy for a month!"	"That candy sure looks good, but candy isn't on our list today."
Your children are fighting over what to watch on TV.	"Please, kids, can't you be nice to each other? Can't you try to get along?"	"That's it! I've had it! No more TV for the rest of the week. That'll teach you to get along."	"Guys, if you can work out which program to watch, you're welcome to your hour of TV. If not, the TV goes off."
Your daughter left her new bike outside, after you told her not to, and it was stolen.	"Oh, sweetheart. I'm so sorry a bad person took your bike. Don't worry, I promise we'll replace it."	"I warned you not to leave your bike outside, but you wouldn't lis-ten. Now it's gone, and it serves you right."	"I'm sorry your bike was stolen, but you'll be without one for a while. We dis-cussed this ear-lier and agreed that bikes left on the lawn risk being stolen."

(CONTINUED)

■ **What's Your Parenting Style?** **(continued)**

SITUATION	TOO PERMISSIVE	TOO STRICT	SIMPLY AUTHORITATIVE
Your son is begging you for an expensive toy: "Please, Dad, buy me Nintendo. I gotta have it."	"You know we're really strapped for money, but I'll try my best to get it for you just as soon as I can."	"Look at all the stuff you already have. You're never satisfied. Think of the poor kids who have nothing."	"That sure does look like a neat toy. I can see why you'd like to have it. But you'll have to put it on your wish list for now."

Too Strict

The authoritarian approach isn't any better. The overly strict parent takes control and expects unquestioning obedience. Being too authoritarian means exacting obedience from children at all costs. Children don't always require an explanation, nor do they have to like your rule. But when you say, "The answer is no because I said so," it's the same as saying, "How dare you question my authority? Who do you think you are?" That's a familiar script many of us adults remember unpleasantly from our own childhoods.

Authoritarian child rearing breeds defiance and sneakiness. The following example illustrates an authoritarian approach to the previous situation of calling Kevin in for bed:

> **Mom:** Kevin, you'd better come in here this minute!
> **Kevin:** Just half an hour more.
> **Mom:** No! You get in this house now, or else.
> **Kevin:** *(whining)* I want to stay out . . .
> **Mom:** When I say now, I mean *now.*

Mom starts to approach Kevin angrily. As she reaches to grab his arm and pull him into the house, he dodges her grip. Mom warns, "If you don't get in here, I won't let you go out after supper for the rest of the summer!"

Better: Be Authoritative

Authoritative parents understand the need to set limits and provide structure for their children. But in the process, they treat their children the way they themselves would like to be treated: with respect and dignity.

The scene between Kevin and his mom looks very different when she takes an authoritative approach. Before Kevin went outside, he and his mom agreed that he would come in at eight o'clock. That agreement forms the basis for calling him to come in:

> **Mom:** Kevin, it's eight o'clock.
> **Kevin:** Already? I've only been out for a little while.
> **Mom:** I know. But the clock says eight.

Kevin comes in reluctantly, and he complains a bit, but Mom doesn't take it personally. She's not ambivalent about her decision. Instead, she says, "I don't blame you for being disappointed, but that was our agreement." Knowing it's pointless to argue, Kevin finds something else to do.

I like the way Barbara Coloroso, in her book *Kids Are Worth It* (Avon Books, 1995), describes these three parenting styles. She calls them "jellyfish," "brick wall," and "backbone."

9. Pick Your Battles

For many parents, especially those with small children, daily life seems like an endless series of battles. If you feel like a drill sergeant, if you find that you are barking orders all day long, if you see that your kids tune you out before you've said three words—then you're probably not picking your battles.

It can be difficult to know which battles are important and which are not. One mother, who tried valiantly to balance firmness with flexibility, threw up her hands in dismay. "If I give Nicky an inch, she'll take a mile," she told me.

But it simply doesn't work to fight every battle with equal intensity. In one of my workshops, a father of teens summed up his own experience: "If you're not selective, you're not effective."

Keep Your Perspective

When you find yourself wanting to lay down the law about something or respond rigidly to a given circumstance, it's usually helpful to step back and ask yourself how much it really matters. Parents in my workshops often find that they're able to become more flexible when they ask themselves questions like these:

- Will it matter a week from now if Eric doesn't finish his dinner tonight?
- How important is it whether or not Eileen wears purple nail polish?
- Will there be serious consequences if John plays outside for an extra half hour?
- Will Jenny be safe if she rides her bike to the corner store?
- If Jill forgets to take her lunch to school, what's the worst thing that'll happen?

- Can I let it go when Javier wears an outfit to school that I think looks completely ridiculous?

Let's face it. It's impractical and counterproductive to make rules for every occasion. Better to allow some slack when the consequences aren't grave. A parent I met recently told me she makes the big decisions and lets her three kids make the small decisions. The method works pretty well for her. Another parent, whose creative streak is admirable, asks herself if she'd react with the same intensity if the child were not hers.

A word of advice: It may be hard, but if you practice this balancing act when your children are young, it will be much easier to maintain credibility when they become adolescents.

10. Use Your Power Tools

One of a parent's most critical power tools is the voice of authority. If you can learn to use it in those challenging moments when your child ignores, resists, or simply laughs in the face of your requests, you will significantly diminish the amount of daily conflict that is so exhausting.

Joan, a mother in one of my workshops, complained that she couldn't get her four-year-old son Sam to stop squishing up all the food on his plate into a messy glop. I suggested to her that she might handle the situation by making a simple change in the style of her approach.

To demonstrate this point, I asked Joan to engage in a role-playing scenario with me: "Pretend that I'm Sam, and I'm squishing my food. Respond using the same words and tone of voice you normally use with him."

Joan said in a cajoling voice, "Come on, honey, now please stop playing with your food."

"Why should I?" I replied as Sam. "It's fun, and I like to squish things up."

Joan's voice was firmer, but her words belied authority. "Sam, how about just eating your food, not grinding it till it looks like mush—*OKaaay?*"

After hearing Joan's tone and words, I understood why Sam didn't take her seriously. I pointed out that by adding "OK?" instead of communicating to Sam that his behavior would not be tolerated, she was essentially asking his permission. "You're saying, 'Would it be OK with you?' " I said. "He's going to show you by his actions that it's *not* OK with him. He wants to play. He's having a good time, and he's expecting to get a reaction from you. That's irresistible for a kid." I suggested that a more effective response would be to issue a short, clear warning: "Eat the food as it is, or I'll remove it." I urged her to use her power voice—not shouting or angry, but clear and no-nonsense.

Without realizing it, many parents come across as wishy-washy by stating their demands as questions:

"Now, put your pj's on . . . OK?"
"Would you mind setting the table?"
"How about turning off the TV and helping to put these groceries away?"
"I'd like you to be home by four o'clock . . . alright?"

Parents betray a lack of confidence in their authority when they *ask* instead of *state* their expectations. Compare the preceding questions to the following statements, delivered in a polite but firm tone of voice:

"It's time to put your pj's on."

"I need you to set the table now."

"Please turn off the television and help me with these groceries."

"I expect you home by four o'clock."

Keep your power voice on hand as an indispensable item in your bag of parenting tools. It will minimize the battles, subdue the nagging, and end the begging—both theirs and yours.

PART 2

■

Minimize Daily Stresses

11. End Morning Madness

For many of us, mornings are the worst part of the day. By the time we've gotten the kids up, dressed, fed, and finally out the door, we're exhausted—and the day has barely begun. When I give a speech, I often ask the parents in the audience, "How many of you said, 'Hurry up, come on,' at least thirty times this morning?" A majority of hands go up. But with the following strategies, you *can* lighten your load and lessen the chaos.

Start on a Positive Note

Your first words of the day set the tone. If you're racing around, issuing loud wake-up calls, and shouting orders, don't be surprised if your children are cranky and uncooperative. On the other hand, a smile and a soft touch can go a long way toward making a hectic morning go much more smoothly. One mom plays a favorite tune or sings to her kids as a wake-up ritual.

Of course, it's not always easy to be chipper and pleasant, especially on days when your child won't even get out of bed or you yourself are sleep-deprived. But even if you momentarily lose it, the whole morning isn't necessarily doomed. For days that get off to a bad start, I suggest the handy "erase" technique. Try saying, "Let's start all over again. Time to get up, my little sleepyhead."

Get Ready the Night Before

You can save time and anxiety in the morning by being more organized the night before. Get your children involved in laying out their clothes for the next day. One mom, whose daughter would change her mind every morning, no matter what had been picked the night before, rearranged her child's closet and drawers so that very few items were available. It worked!

Let your children help you prepare lunch. They can spread peanut butter on bread, mash up the tuna, and wrap the celery and carrot sticks. When children feel as though they are involved and useful, they are more likely to be cooperative.

To solve last-minute panic attacks over misplaced items, pinpoint the chronic problems. For instance, if your three-year-old consistently can't find her shoes, you may want to designate a regular spot for her to place them at night before the lights go out. If your second-grader tends to leave his homework on the floor, suggest that he put it in his knapsack as soon as he's finished with his assignment. Another way to make sure nothing is missed is to pile essential items in front of the door so that you have to trip over them to get out of the house.

Make a Checklist

If items often get left behind in the mad dash to get out the door, create a written checklist for these items. Make sure the list is displayed in a prominent place so that everyone can see it. One mother told me that she used a checklist to help her child stop dawdling in the morning. Instead of nagging him about getting ready to go, together they made up a list that specified all of his morning routines to be completed. It included getting dressed, brushing his teeth, feeding his pet gerbil, eating breakfast, and packing his lunch. As soon as each task was completed, he'd run to the list to check the box. The mother stopped feeling like a nag, and the morning rush became smoother and less stressful.

Offer Choices

One way to encourage your child to cooperate in the morning is to offer limited choices. For example, when your headstrong three-year-old dawdles in the morning, instead of saying, "Hurry up" or "C'mon" thirty times, you could say: "What dress are you going to wear today?" or "What color are you in the mood for?" This works because instead of pushing your child to hurry and get going, she feels like she has some say in the matter.

If your five-year-old tells you he doesn't want to brush his teeth, you might reply, "Well, you can choose to brush your teeth yourself or I'll brush them for you." That usually works if offered as an option, not a threat. A parent I know has a more playful style. He says to his three-year-old, "As soon as you brush *your* teeth, then you can brush mine."

Keep Breakfast Simple

Breakfast can be a real source of friction. It goes without saying that the most coveted cereal is in the box that's almost empty. And the least-favorite food is the one you've already prepared. Avoid some of these battles by placing less significance on this meal and not pressuring your kids to eat.

One strategy is to keep it simple. Even if your mother always served you a hot breakfast, let's face it: Cold cereal is easier. And some days, even cereal may take too much time. One mother told me, somewhat guiltily, "We were running so late last week that I gave my daughter a chicken drumstick left over from dinner the night before to eat in the car." I told her to save her guilt for more serious transgressions. Actually, I found this to be a rather creative

■ Countdown to Blastoff!

Once you get organized, NASA will have nothing on you when it comes to preparing for takeoff.

Strategic Planning

Time yourself daily until you have accurately assessed how much time you need to get out of the house. Example: "To get my kids from bedcovers to car seats takes sixty minutes, plus I need at least thirty minutes of my own time."

Early-Warning System

Deploy a stove-top timer to count down the minutes available to get things done. Try using five- or ten-minute intervals, and focus on one task at a time. Example: "You have five minutes to use the bathroom and put on your coats. Can you beat the clock today?"

Launching Pad

Install a long, low row of hooks right by the door, where children can hang their gear. Don't place more than two garments on a hook. Below the coat rack, give each child a color-coded container for damp boots, car toys, and other travel essentials. The child's coat hook can also be used to hold a tote bag. Keep off-season jackets and infrequently used outerwear in another closet or an inaccessible spot.

Reentry Program

Your launching pad will work only if you help your kids get in the habit of hanging up their gear when they walk in the door. Be sure to set a good example yourself!

---

solution. Eating on the run may not be ideal, but it's certainly nothing to agonize over. There are plenty of portable, car-friendly foods for kids three and over, such as a granola bar and an apple, or juice in a box and a bagel.

When all else fails, give thanks for weekends—those lovely two days when you often don't have to deal with time crunches. Try not to schedule appointments, errands, or play dates for an entire morning, so you can all dawdle to your hearts' content. You can also take comfort in the fact that as your kids grow older, they'll be able to do more for themselves, which will make mornings less hectic. In fact, in just a few years, the shoe may be on the other foot, with your child tapping his foot impatiently at the door, saying, "Come on, Mom, I've got choir practice. Hurry, or I'm going to be late!"

12. Eliminate Food Fights

Whenever the topic of food comes up in my groups, it is met with a giant moan of frustration, helplessness, and anxiety. Parents invest so much emotional energy in trying to get their children to eat, and children oblige by being picky, obstinate, and "not hungry."

Here are nine strategies to help eliminate food fights in your home:

1. **Relax traditional food/mealtime selections.** A slice of pizza, an egg-salad sandwich cut into triangles, or even last night's leftovers might be more appealing for breakfast than the standard cereal and banana. Both my sons loved spaghetti for breakfast—either leftovers from the night before or freshly boiled.

    When I hear from parents who either pretend to be indifferent or are truly not that concerned about every morsel their children eat or refuse to eat, I know those are the parents who will avoid daily battles at mealtimes. And you really can't *make* kids eat nor can you control their hunger—or lack of it. (Have you ever tried to get a baby to drink more milk than she wants?) So try to avoid power struggles over food. It's a losing proposition.

2. **Don't assume she's hungry just because it's mealtime.** Before putting food in front of your child, ask, "Are you hungry?" If she says no, take her seriously. If you try to make her eat when she doesn't want to, she won't learn how to recognize her own hunger signals.

3. **Focus less on what she eats in the course of a day.** Instead, consider what she eats over a period of a week. She may be eating a very small portion at each meal, but overall, she's probably getting as much food as she needs.

4. **Serve *much* smaller portions.** For example, if you typically give your three-year-old daughter three squares of ravioli, reduce that to one and then divide it into four pieces. If she wants more, she can always have seconds.

■ **Parent's Story: One Potato, Two Potato**

When talking about trying to get kids to eat nutritionally balanced meals, especially whole wheat and vegetables, one dad recalled that when he was seven, he ate only one potato for dinner every night for weeks—and nothing else! He was a healthy kid, and now he's a healthy adult. Another parent said that she was allowed to eat Cheerios for every meal for almost two years. "Not being pressured to eat made mealtime a lot more pleasant," she noted. She, too, survived and eventually outgrew her limited menu.

---

5. **Don't push her to take "just one more bite" to please you.** Children naturally tune into their own feelings of hunger—unless you talk them out of it. Avoid the "clean plate club" or the "starving children" remonstrations. In spite of what our parents preached, finishing our veggies never changed the course of hunger in the world.

6. **Don't make a big deal out of your child's pickiness.** Often parents will resort to any number of ploys—including threatening, bribing, begging, or devoting vast amounts of time to finding just the foods they hope will please their finicky child's palate, only to have their efforts fail.

7. **Introduce new foods gradually.** Ask whether your child wants to try something different, and if he says he doesn't, don't react negatively. Say, "Oh, I guess you're not ready to try baked potatoes." A parent I know has been successful with reverse psychology, saying, "You can't even have a taste. This is adult food." Suddenly her normally picky son must have the asparagus!

8. **Don't bribe with dessert.** One parent I know refuses to use dessert as a reward to bribe her children to eat. Instead, she serves dessert every day at 4:00 P.M. as an after-school treat. Think about it. Does it make any sense to reward a child for eating an extra bite of broccoli so he can qualify for dessert? Eating broccoli doesn't constitute doing anything thoughtful, kind, or virtuous!

9. **Know that this, too, will pass.** As a wise father in one of my workshops told a mother who was worried about her son's single-minded devotion to canned spaghetti, "How many twenty-five-year-old men do you know who even like canned spaghetti—much less eat it exclusively?"

Parent's Story:"Eat Your Browns"

Sometimes cooking with your child can provide an incentive to eat. One mother, very into "brown food" (whole wheat, brown rice, etc.) asked her six-year-old son to help her make bran muffins from scratch. All went well until it was time to add the molasses, whereupon the child made loud gagging sounds and said, "That smells like gasoline and poop!"

Great beginning. But next time, why not omit the molasses?

13. Win the Bedtime Wars

Getting three-year-old Julie to go to bed on time was a constant struggle. As her weary mom, Helen, described it, every night was filled with escalating dramatics and loud demands for "just one more"—minute, story, drink of water, back rub, kiss. Long after the lights were out, Julie was still calling from her room: "Mommy, I need you to come here." "Mommy, I'm scared." "Mommy, I'm thirsty."

Few kids like to go to bed. The same child who one minute whines, "I'm too tired to clean up," is suddenly wide awake and energized at bedtime. If you've nearly lost hope that a peaceful bedtime transition is possible, try these strategies.

Give Advance Notice

Instead of announcing, "Time's up," give a ten-minute warning when TV watching is coming to an end—and follow through. Or you might say in advance, "It will be time to put on your pj's soon.

If you'd rather take your bath right now, we'll have time for two stories tonight. If you'd prefer to play for fifteen minutes before your bath, I can read only one story. You decide."

When Time Is Up, Be Firm

Many parents feel guilty about enforcing a strict bedtime because they already feel they don't spend enough time with their kids. But parents have a legitimate need for some adult time alone. Bear in mind that you'll be a more effective parent if you have an opportunity to get a good night's sleep. You've said good night and gone through the ritual. Let your child know that once you've kissed him good night, he must stay in his room. One mom told her daughter, "This is Dad and Mom's time to have a play date."

Don't Try to Force Sleep

While you can insist that your child stay in his room and not disturb you, you can't force a child to go to sleep. You might say, "After I kiss you good night, it's my time to be with Daddy. You can play quietly with your toys, look at a book, or listen to relaxing music, but you have to stay in your room." Or if you're a

---

■ **Parent's Story: The PJ Ploy**

When three-year-old Molly declared, "I'm not going to put on my pj's—*ever*," her Mom was tempted to respond with a threat. She always felt so helpless when Molly dug in her heels and refused to cooperate. This time she tried a different approach. Ignoring Molly's statement, she merely said, "If you get your pj's on now, we'll be able to read a story before bed." Stated simply and objectively, Molly soon appeared with her pj's on.

---

single parent, "It's my time for me." Your child will be more likely to stay put if you give him some control over his environment. For example, if he wants to wear sweats instead of pajamas or sleep in a tent erected on the bedroom floor, humor him. You can also provide him with nighttime "props" to keep him quietly entertained—such as a flashlight or a tape that plays his favorite stories.

Establish an Understanding About Privacy

One common dilemma parents face is whether to let children sleep in the bed with them. It may have already become a habit during an illness or a spate of bad dreams. There is no one right answer to the question of whether to let kids sleep in your bed. I believe parents have to decide that for themselves. What I ask them is, "How strongly do *you* feel about this? What would *you* like to do?" Some parents are comfortable with the idea of the "family bed." If it works for you, that's perfectly OK. But do it only if you want to—not because you feel pressured by your child. And it's absolutely crucial that both spouses agree on this! Most parents just don't want their kids in bed with them. They may feel it's too crowded, that a restless child keeps them awake, or that they simply want their privacy.

The alternative, however, is not to drag your child into her room and shut the door while she cries in misery. If your child is sleeping with you and you want her to sleep on her own in her bed, try making the change gradually. You might start with a sleeping bag on the floor next to your bed, then move it into the hall, and then into her own room. Most kids eventually prefer their own beds as they master the process of separation.

While it's tempting to let your child come into your bed when she's scared, try to comfort her in her own room, not in yours. If she has had a frightening dream, you can sit quietly with her until she feels better. Ask if she wants a light left on, a drink of water, or a cuddly toy to keep her company.

Ultimately, your goal is to prevent bedtime from becoming a nightly battle. Then your child can develop good sleep habits, and you can have time alone or an early bedtime—whichever you need the most!

14. Survive the Supermarket

Perched in the seat of a shopping cart, two-and-a-half-year-old Jeffrey tightly grasped a candy bar he had plucked from the shelf. His mother, trying to reason with him, pleaded, "Come on, Jeffrey, honey, put the candy back, please. Will you do that for Mommy?" He responded like a typical toddler: "No. I *waaant* it."

Jeffrey's mom shot a quick glance of embarrassment at the sea of shoppers watching her attentively and tried again. "Please, sweetie. Now give the candy to Mommy." He held it tighter to his chest. "No. Mine!"

Finally, she lost patience and pried the candy bar from Jeffrey's iron-fisted fingers while he kicked his legs against the cart and howled.

Why is food shopping such a hotbed of stress and struggle for parents and young children? Well, from a child's point of view, the supermarket is a wild kaleidoscope of colors, sounds, smells, and sensations. The colorful rows of produce, the fragrances from the bakery, and the long aisles of notebooks, crayons, squirt guns, and action figures present an irresistible temptation. And your child sees big people sniffing melons, squeezing bread, tasting grapes, and grabbing jars off the shelves. So why can't he? Expecting a young child to remain calm in this environment is as unrealistic as taking him to the circus and expecting him to doze off.

Accept the fact that if you're going to take children shopping, you can't expect to breeze in and out in less than thirty minutes. However, there are ways of teaching your child appropriate super-market behavior and even having fun in the process:

- Invent letter and number games to distract your five-year-old. Ask her to count up the number of orange boxes on a shelf or tell you how many letters she recognizes on a package.
- Enlist your four-year-old's help in finding items you need on the shelves. Say, "Please look for the can with the pic-ture of peas," and, "Hand Mommy the blue box." Ask, "Can you find the brand of orange juice we use?"
- An eight-year-old can bring a pocket calculator to add up the items as they go into the cart. Tell her, "Be sure to let me know when we reach thirty dollars."
- Ask your five-year-old to help you make decisions. Say, "We only have enough money to buy one kind of cereal. You decide. Shall it be Cheerios or Wheat Chex?"
- Your six-year-old can hold the grocery list and read it off as you go.
- If you're lucky enough to shop in a market that has child-sized carts, you'll find that shopping is much less stressful. Your preschooler can feel more grown-up by becoming an active participant.

Check It Out

The average weekly shopping expedition lasts about forty-five minutes. Even if there's just one person in front of you, you'll probably be in the checkout lane for ten to fifteen minutes of that time, according to Martin Sloane, author of the syndicated column "Supermarket Shopper." Given that a typical toddler's attention span is a fraction of that, it's no wonder that this last stop is often the biggest hurdle. Here are some survival strategies for the checkout line:

- Talk to the manager about establishing at least one candy- and gum-free checkout lane. Some stores already offer this amenity, as the result of a parent or a group of parents asking for a family-friendly zone.
- Let your child pick out a coloring or activity book while you're shopping. Tell her she can play with it while standing in line. Or bring a book or portable toy from home specifically for the line.
- Let your six-year-old help put the groceries in a bag. Granted, she won't do as good a job as you or the cashier would, but as long as she's not handling the eggs or other fragile items, she can't do much harm. You could also let your child hand items or coupons to the cashier.

When the outing does go well, be sure to praise your child for doing a good job. You might say, "Thank you! You were such a big help to me." Pay special attention to improved behavior and be sure to comment on it. For example, you might say, "I noticed the effort you made not to touch things, even though it must have been so tempting."

Solutions to Shopping Pitfalls

Many parents of young children encounter the following pitfalls. If any of these situations sound familiar, then try the suggested solutions:

- **Your toddler won't stay in the cart.**

  Don't: Engage in a power struggle at the moment your child is trying to crawl out. Toddlers can have wills of steel when they want their freedom.

  Do: Establish that she must stay close to you and not run wild. If it's not feasible to let her out of the cart, bring along a toy, doll, or snack to entertain her while you shop.

- **Your child keeps grabbing items off the shelf and putting them in the cart.**

  Don't: Fall into the trap of saying no a hundred times in each aisle. That will exhaust both of you.

  Do: Say in advance, "Can you take the things on our list off the shelf and hand them to me?" If your child grabs for other items, say, "Macaroni isn't on our list today."

- **Your three-year-old whines and begs incessantly during your shopping trips.**

  Don't: Give in to his begging just to keep him quiet.

  Do: Establish before you enter the store that he may pick out one treat or toy, and that's it.

- **Your child is engaged in a full-fledged tantrum in the supermarket aisle.**

  Don't: Try to reason with him, bribe him, or throw a tantrum yourself.

  Do: Try to stay calm. Get out of the store if necessary. Go over the ground rules for store behavior later, after he has calmed down.

15. Tame the TV

Before my first child was born, I watched one of my nephews plopped in front of the TV set in a slack-jawed trance. If I tried to talk to him, he wouldn't answer—he was literally tuned out. The sight left a deep impression on me, so when I sensed that television had begun to take on too much importance in my sons' lives, I called a family meeting. I told the boys that there would be a new rule about TV. TV watching would be allowed only on the weekends. I explained my reasons and listened to their questions and objections. But they could see how strongly I felt about this and that I was not about to be pressured into changing my mind. To my surprise, they accepted the rule much less grudgingly than I had expected.

Here are some suggestions for taming the TV in your home.

Reinforce Your Values

Watch TV with your kids, and use the opportunity to get your values across by expressing opinions indirectly. For example, comment on the behavior of a TV character: "Seems she's being awfully irresponsible about her friend's safety." Or, "Those kids are bullying that boy. What do you think he should do?"

If there's a controversial movie your kids are dying to see, watch it with them (even if they don't yearn for your presence), and later ask their opinion about it. If you have any doubt that the content is appropriate for your children, check it out. When you view a TV show or movie with older children, don't lecture them about how violent or immoral the movie is, but ask them what they think about characters' actions and decisions. You could ask casually, "Does that situation sound realistic? Would you recommend this movie? If so, why? What would you do in that situation?" Questions like these will draw them out, give you an insight into their thinking, and help get your values across—as long as you're not preaching at them and you really listen when they answer.

Limit TV Hours

You don't have to go to the extreme of banning TV completely. What you *do* need to do is limit how much and what your kids watch—especially younger children. Because TV has had such a harmful effect on children's mental and physical health, the American Academy of Pediatrics recommends that children under age two not watch TV at all, and older children be limited to a maximum of ten hours a week. Although I encourage parents to keep television sets out of their children's bedrooms, many parents obviously disagree. According to the Kaiser Family Foundation, 53 percent of children have a TV in their room.

Hold Your Ground

When Marilyn would not allow her eight-year-old daughter to watch a television program that she considered too violent, her daughter reacted angrily. "Jennifer made me feel like the worst mother in the world," Marilyn recalled. "She claimed she was the only one in her class who wasn't allowed to watch that program. Everybody was talking about it. She felt left out and stupid. She called me mean and said I treated her like a baby."

This can be a trying moment for a parent. You're motivated by love, but your child thinks you're hateful. This mother thought it might help to explain to her daughter why the program was out of bounds in their house. It was something of a fool's errand. The more she explained, the harder Jennifer fought to get her mother to change her mind. I urged this mother to state the rule clearly, without trying to explain, and see what happened. The following conversation resulted:

Jennifer: You're just being mean. Everyone gets to watch it except me. You don't want me to have any friends.
Mom: We don't watch violent television programs in this house.
Jennifer: Please, Mom!
Mom: Jennifer, I know you'd like me to relent, but I'm standing firm. Watching that program is *not* an option.

Sometimes, you just have to state your decision and then stand tough, in spite of your child's misery. Your child may be furious, but you need to exercise your authority just the same.

Cultivate a Love for Reading

Don't buy into the multimedia hype. I hear many parents expressing the opinion that books have already lost the war against electronic entertainment. These parents assume that, given a choice, children will always pick TV, movies, computers, and electronic games over books. I disagree. There has never before been such a varied and exciting marketplace of books for kids of all ages. And the books are selling!

I've also discovered that when a child loves to read, he *will* read, no matter what else is going on. I was impressed by the story of one child who so loved Roald Dahl's book *James and the Giant Peach* that he refused to see the movie version. "I already imagined all the characters," he said. "I don't want them to be spoiled." And I was thrilled with the extraordinary *Harry Potter* phenomenon, which proved children can still be turned on by the magic of books, even in our high-tech world where so many kids seem permanently attached to a screen.

I believe that a love of reading is one of the greatest gifts we can give our children. Jim Trelease, author of *The Read-Aloud Handbook* (Penguin, revised 2001), has taught countless parents, teachers, and administrators to help kids fall in love with books. To parents who claim they're too busy to read to their children, he writes: "If Americans were out of time, the video stores would be in bankruptcy, you'd have only ten TV channels (one set to a house), and the mall parking lot would be three-quarters empty. We have time for what we value. The people who found the time to read to a child . . . had the same 24 hours as the person who had no time . . . but did watch their favorite team on TV or the afternoon soap they taped, did find the time to talk on the phone for 35 minutes . . . and the time to run over to the mall for an errand."

Taming the TV is an uphill battle that demands more of parents than many of them are willing to invest. However, countless studies have summed up the relationship of TV to academic success with the following fact that might help motivate all of us to put more limits on the amount of time devoured by the tube: Those who watch the most, achieve the least in school.

16. Don't Get Caught in the World Wide Web

Today parents are faced with ever-expanding techno-terrors. It's not just the TV anymore. It's the computer and video games, too. And while the television fare of my sons' youth was merely mind numbing, today's menu includes graphic sex and violence—not to mention the serious dangers kids face from real, live predators.

Parents have to be especially vigilant, state the rules clearly and firmly, and reinforce their values often.

The following suggestions will help give you a handle on this very difficult dilemma:

- **Keep it out in the open.** Don't put a computer in your child's bedroom. Why? Because if you do, you lose all control. Kids may want to play video games and surf the Net all day, but this is passive and isolating—and you can't monitor their exposure.

- **Control their access.** Keep a watch on what your kids are doing on the computer, especially when they're on the Internet. Pornography, hate, and violence are pandemic. Even with Net Nanny and other blocking software, kids today are so computer savvy that they can often circumvent your best efforts. You have to pay attention. Put the computer in the family room or den where everyone has access and where you can talk with them—and they can talk with you—about what they're doing online.

- **Stay in charge.** Even though our high-tech universe is galloping faster than anyone can imagine, you still have to be the one in charge, not your children. Expecting them to limit their access to all the exciting new electronic devices is like asking them to show restraint when left alone in a toy store. Mimi Doe, in *Busy But Balanced* (Griffin Trade Paperback, 2001), has many suggestions for enhancing family intimacy away from the ubiquitous screen. One tip: "Create a 'no-technology time' in your house and turn off the computers, DVDs, Gameboys, TVs, phones, beepers, Playstations, fax machines, and Walkmans. How great for your kids to 'get bored'—that's where creativity flows in, that's where their inner voice can finally be heard."

Following is a list of important tips for parents to help their children use the Internet safely:

- Ensure your children don't spend all of their free time on the computer. Have them interact with other people, not just a computer.
- Keep the computer in a visible, high-traffic area of your home.
- Learn how to use and operate the computer yourself.
- See where your children go while they're online—surf the Net together.
- Make sure your kids feel comfortable coming to you with questions.
- Keep your kids out of unmonitored chat rooms or IRCs (Internet relay chats).
- Encourage discussions between you and your children about their online activities.
- Discuss these rules with your children.
- Help your children find a balance between the computer and other activities.
- Get to know their "online friends" just as you would get to know all of their other friends.
- Warn them that people might not be what they seem.
- Remember to monitor their compliance with these rules.
- Don't store passwords or credit card information on your computer.
- Check the cache, history, and downloaded files every so often on your computer(s). Let your children know you will be doing this.

Adapted from *The Parent's Guide to Protecting Your Child in Cyberspace*, by Parry Aftab (McGraw-Hill Professional Publishing, 1999).

17. Make Chores Matter

One of the frequent complaints I hear from parents is that kids today aren't doing chores the way their parents remember doing them when they were young. This constant source of frustration causes parents to nag and kids to resist or ignore them. However, sometimes we parents can get stuck on the issues of neatness and chores to the exclusion of other values. In fact, when they think about it, most parents would probably agree that it is not a healthy sign when a child is obsessed with being neat. Imagine how you would react if your child walked into the kitchen and exclaimed, "Hey, Mom, this place is full of dirty pots and pans. Let me scrub them right away for you."

Kids rarely share our passion for neatly made beds or floors that aren't littered with toys. They just don't seem preoccupied by the messes they make or share our sense of urgency for cleanup. When we constantly bug them to "make your bed . . . pick up your toys . . . take out the trash," most children tend to be uncooperative or resistant.

No, I'm not saying chores are unimportant or irrelevant. What I do advocate is putting their importance in perspective.

Make the Connection

Since children learn important values from being helpful, we can make the most of their genuine desire to feel needed by establishing a connection between their doing a chore and making a real contribution to the life of the family. Even children as young as two can sort colors, match socks, put clothes in the hamper, help collect and throw out papers, and use the Dustbuster to help you clean up. At that age they love "working" alongside you and haven't yet realized that chores can be tedious. Preschoolers and kindergartners can help with simple food preparation, learn to set the table, rake leaves, use the dustpan, or sweep. Elementary school kids can tutor younger siblings, in addition to learning how to use the dishwasher and washing machine.

Children soon grasp the difference between superficially imposed chores—"busy work"—and tasks that are meaningful. For example, if you ask your daughter to pick up a quart of milk on the way home from school because you have to work late and won't have time to go to the market, she can easily see that this chore meets a real need: milk for dinner and for cereal in the morning. On the other hand, she might view making her bed or neatly folding clothes before putting them in drawers as busy work that doesn't achieve any meaningful purpose.

One mother tried to make that connection with her preschooler, who complained and stalled whenever it was time to clean up the many toys, puzzles, and books that were scattered all over the floor:

> **Mom:** Ronnie, can you see a reason why I bug you to clean up the playroom?
>
> **Ronnie:** Yeah. Because you like to bug me.
>
> **Mom:** Hmmm. Does your preschool teacher ask you to pick up your toys when you're finished playing?
>
> **Ronnie:** Yes . . .
>
> **Mom:** Gee, I wonder what would happen if nobody picked up toys at preschool.
>
> **Ronnie:** *(laughing)* They'd pile up to the ceiling! We couldn't even get in there!

To reinforce the message when children are small, you can make simple connections between tasks and benefits. For example, you might say, "Please put the juice back in the refrigerator so it won't spoil." Even better, ask them what they think will happen if a task is neglected: "What do you think would happen to the ice cream if we forgot to put it in the freezer? . . . the crumbs if they were left on the table overnight? . . . the dishes if we didn't wash them?"

But don't keep repeating your order. Ask once, make the consequences plain, then allow your child to experience those consequences. If the juice stays out on the counter overnight, you can say, "I know you love your juice in the morning, but the juice is spoiled because it wasn't put back in the refrigerator last night."

Don't Forget to Say Thanks

We all like to hear that our actions have made another person's life easier or happier. Kids are no different. When they pitch in, let them know you appreciate it. Try to be specific in your praise— not just "You're *such* a help" but "When you help me do the dishes, it goes so much faster, and we have more time to read together."

Whenever possible, reinforce in words that the chore really does make a significant difference, enabling your kids to see the family as a place where people pitch in to help one another.

18. Turn the Frowns Upside Down

All children get in bad moods now and then. If you're having a rough day yourself, it can be trying to listen to the moaning, groaning, and complaining. But you can make your life easier while easing your child's angst by dealing skillfully with bad moods. The following situations are typical of bad-mood moments parents experience with their children, along with practical and simple ways to handle them.

Situation 1: "Nobody Likes Me"

Your seven-year-old daughter is moping around the house. When you ask her what's wrong, she responds with a whine, "Nobody likes me."

> **Ineffective Reaction:** You may believe this statement to be groundless since she's usually very social, and your first reaction may be to say, "Don't be absurd! You have lots of friends." However, your daughter will certainly not be reassured, and she'll probably be annoyed with you for not giving any credence to her complaint.

> **What You *Can* Do:** Explore what's really going on. Why is your daughter feeling so upset? What happened to make her state so emphatically that nobody likes her? Sometimes complaints are an oblique way to elicit feedback. By not denying her words, you give her the opportunity to use you as a sounding board. For example, you might reply sympathetically, "You look so sad." This will open the door for her to tell you what's on her mind. And nothing defuses a bad mood more than empathy.

Situation 2: "I'm Bored"

Lately, it seems that your eight-year-old son is always in a bad mood about something. He often sulks and complains about being bored. No matter what you suggest, he rejects it, saying, "That's boring" or "I don't want to do that."

Ineffective Reaction: You keep suggesting activities, hoping you'll find one that he accepts. When that doesn't work, you get so frustrated that you resort to threats, such as, "If you don't snap out of it, I'm going to cancel our trip to the zoo this weekend."

Trying to find something your child finds interesting can be a drag on your time and patience. Sometimes bored moods are just bored moods. Threats never help to change a child's mood for the better. More likely, they'll make him more confrontational and increase the sulking.

What You *Can* Do: Remove yourself from the situation. It's not your job to be the entertainment director for your kids. When I was a child, my mother used this strategy to great effect. I could sometimes get in a sulky mood, and my mother was not particularly tolerant of that. She would say, "Just because you're in a bad mood, that doesn't mean I'm going to join you. Why don't you come back when you feel better?"

My mother's approach worked. She wasn't ordering me to stop sulking. She was telling me I could sulk all I wanted, just not in her presence. Since my main reason for sulking was to get her attention, I wasn't so motivated to be grumpy.

Situation 3: Power Struggle on the Horizon

Your four-year-old is mad at you. She wants to go outside and play, but you've told her that she has to put away her toys first. You can sense a power struggle looming as soon as you see her stormy face.

Ineffective Reaction: You're frustrated. Why can't she just do what you say, so you can get on with the day? You tell her, "If you had started picking up your toys ten minutes ago when I first asked you, you'd be outside playing by now."

While this may make perfect sense to you, it's already too late, and your four-year-old won't grasp the logic. In fact, it may cause her to dig in her heels.

What You *Can* Do: Realize that an apparently simple task like picking up toys can seem overwhelming and endless for a four-year-old. Lighten up yourself by making a game out of what feels to her like a chore. For example, you could set a timer and say, "Let's have a race. I'll pick up the books, and you put the dirty clothes in the hamper, and we'll see who finishes first."

Even when you do respond in a helpful way, as these examples have suggested, don't expect that bad moods will always disappear like magic. Not every situation is that simple. Sometimes time is the best cure. However, if you take that extra moment to pause and be sensitive to what your child is experiencing at that instant, you can go a long way toward turning a frown upside down.

Watch Your Own Moods

Don't forget—children model our behavior. If we tend to complain a lot and are easily agitated by mundane disappointments, chances are our children will mimic our act. The reverse is also true. For example, imagine the following situations:

- **The plumber didn't show up when he was supposed to, and you had to wait all morning.**

  Don't Say: "Now he's ruined my whole day."
  Do Say: "It's so annoying when people don't show up for an appointment you've scheduled."

- **A teller at the bank is rude to you.**

  Don't Say: "How dare she speak to me that way! I'm going to report her to the manager."
  Do Say: "I guess she's having a bad day."

- **Your friend cancels a lunch date.**

  Don't Say: "She obviously doesn't care about me or my needs."
  Do Say: "I'm disappointed not to see her, but we can reschedule our date."

19. Jump-Start the Dawdler

Dawdling comes as naturally to young kids as breathing. While parents tend to focus on the future and getting things done, young children live in the moment and are totally absorbed in what they're doing. When you command your child to hurry up, it barely registers as more than background noise.

Kids simply don't share our urgency about schedules or getting to places on time. After all, young kids can't even tell time, much less keep track of it. Many children struggle with transitions, especially when they involve separation. Saying good-bye to parents and friends is hard for them, even if they like going to preschool or are looking forward to a snack once they get home. Though kids don't deliberately put a crimp in our carefully planned schedules, dawdling is their way of moving through time. It's also a way of feeling in control and getting us to focus on them.

What's the solution? If you can meet your child halfway, you'll gain a lot toward meeting your own needs, too—and it may not even take that much time. Here are seven ways to do this:

- **Be understanding.** Acknowledge that what your child is doing is important to her. Tell her, "I wish we had more time to play with your dolls. It looks like fun. But right now, your friends are waiting for you at school."

- **Remove obstacles.** Sometimes kids can't get going because they're overwhelmed by too many choices. If it takes your child too long to choose a bedtime story, clear out the titles he never asks for and donate them to the library or the local children's hospital. That will help him to focus on a few favorites.

- **Give a warning.** Children who are busy doing something cannot stop on a dime. Being able to anticipate an event helps them switch gears. Give your child a gentle reminder that he has five more minutes to put his blocks away and then set an egg timer. When the bell goes off, it's time to wrap up the activity.

- **Play beat-the-clock.** For younger children, use the timer to race against time. Tell your toddler or preschooler, "I bet you can't wash your face, get into your pj's, and get under the covers before the timer goes off." Chances are he'll try to get everything done in no time flat.

- **Offer options.** Let's say your two-year-old doesn't want to stop watching a video, even though the family needs to leave for Grandma's. Tell her that there are two ways to get to the car: hopping on one foot or being carried by you. Given the choice, she'll probably hop to it.

- **Turn the tables.** Let your child be the one to get *you* going. Instead of trying to awaken her five-year-old son out of bed every morning, one mother bought him his own alarm clock and instructed him to wake her up when it went off. It worked like a charm. As soon as he got the chance to be in charge, he stopped dragging his feet.

- **Go with the flow.** Once in a while, put your agenda on hold. Instead of hurrying your child home from the park, let her swing until *she* says it's time to go. Try saying something you may have rarely said before, such as, "Sweetie, take all the time you need. I'm not in a hurry today." If you occasionally let your child set the pace, she's more likely to cooperate when your plans don't mesh with hers.

20. Practice Consistency

In a perfect world, we parents would always be completely consistent about our rules. But life with children is messy, and parents are only human. Consistency is a wonderful goal. You're obviously going to be more effective if you don't announce a rule one day and bend it the next. However, when you're exhausted, upset, distracted, or angry, rules are harder to enforce.

The key to consistency is managing to avoid moments when exasperation or fatigue drives you to give in with the useless caveat "just this once." For example, Myra had a firm rule that eight-year-old Janet was not allowed to walk to the store by herself. Janet didn't like this rule, because she wanted to be more independent, but Myra didn't feel comfortable allowing her daughter to cross the busy street between their home and the store. However, one day when Myra was busy with a sick baby and Janet kept nagging her, she agreed because she didn't have the strength to argue. "You can go," she told Janet, "but this is the only time. Don't think I'm going to start letting you do this on a regular basis."

What do you think happened? Once Myra had opened the door, Janet wasn't about to let it close again. The rule was effectively abolished. Myra paid a price for her inconsistency.

Consistency is especially important in the day-to-day routines. Predictable routines help to diminish chaos, especially when several kids are involved. It makes everyone's life easier when the kids not only know what's expected but can count on you to enforce the household rules.

Don't confuse consistency with rigidity. There are going to be times when you may want to make an exception, and you can do it without appearing to be wishy-washy. For example, you might say "Tonight we're going to relax our rule about no TV before bedtime because there is a special on chimpanzees that I think we would all enjoy watching."

It's very hard to be consistent, but our inability to follow through on what we say undermines our credibility with our kids. If we issue idle threats or don't enforce consequences when house rules are broken, our children stop taking us seriously. Many kids even admit that they feel more secure and loved when their parents take the time and trouble to follow through on consequences for clear misbehavior.

There's no question that it's a great goal to "say what you mean and mean what you say," but we all know that it's easier said than done. However, the struggle is worth it. You don't want to be like the parent whose child I overheard saying, "Oh yeah, she always says I'll lose my weekend privileges if I break the curfew, but I can usually talk her out of it!"

Bob, a single dad in my workshop, struggled with being consistent. He admitted that following through was sometimes just too exhausting, especially at the end of a long, stressful workday. When his kids ignored his requests or neglected their chores, he'd get mad and tell them that he was taking TV watching away from them for a week. However, as soon as it was time for their favorite program, they'd apologize and beg and promise that they'd be good. And they were masters of persuasion.

"Come on, Dad, we're really sorry. We promise next time we won't forget again. Please just this once let us watch. Tonight's the last episode of the Simpsons for the whole season."

Dad finally caves in—too tired to fight. "OK, but this is your last chance. Next time you don't do your chores, I'm taking away the TV for two weeks."

"Thanks, Dad, you're the best!" For the moment they're happy and super-affectionate—but his kids have learned that when Dad says no what he really means is "well, maybe."

Meaning what you say is at the basis of being consistent—so if you're not sure how strongly you feel, you're going to have difficulty following through. Stop and think first: is this a threat I am really willing to enforce? To be consistent you've got to feel strongly enough to take on the role of authority. Kids will no longer respect your word if you say yes one day and no the next to the same misbehavior.

21. Establish Rituals and Traditions

I like to call rituals the family comfort zone. These repeated activities, whether a bedtime song or a Saturday-evening phone call to Grandma, help children feel connected and safe. Rituals are the glue that bonds families. Often rituals become the basis for family stories later in life: "Remember how we used to play guessing games at the dinner table?" Many times rituals get passed on from one generation to the next. A father in my workshop described

---

■ Create a Bedtime Ritual

One of the most important daily rituals occurs at bedtime. A bedtime ritual can help your child unwind and reduces anxieties that often surface at bedtime. You might give your daughter a bath, followed by a story. Or play a game, then cuddle in the rocking chair, or sing a favorite song after a back rub. It doesn't really matter what you do, as long as you do it consistently and in the same order. Don't rush through the routine. Skipping pages in the story or bypassing the monster check will only prolong bedtime by drawing protests from your child. Moreover, she'll feel as if she's being shortchanged.

Bedtime rituals can be a precious way of connecting with your child without outside interruptions.

---

how he made French toast for the family on Saturday mornings, just as his father did when he was young.

Sometimes rituals come about from a pleasurable moment. One parent told me how her mother used to wake her up in the morning by singing "You Are My Sunshine." Another parent described the snow day ritual of building a snowman, followed by hot chocolate by the fire. It was one of his most treasured memories. One man described the annual ritual of attending opening day at the baseball stadium, complete with hot dogs and sodas—usually forbidden foods. He has made this an annual outing with his own children. Parents also describe the religious rituals that were so essential to their childhoods—and that they want their own kids to experience—walking to Mass on Sunday mornings or the special Friday-night Sabbath dinner.

Examine the normal course of events, and see if you can identify your family's rituals and traditions. Here are some possibilities to consider:

- Do you have a favorite vacation spot that you visit every summer?
- How does your family celebrate birthdays?
- Is an after-dinner walk part of your summer routine?
- At Christmas, do you take a drive to look at the lights and decorations on people's houses?
- Do you have big holiday dinners with extended family?
- On winter nights, do you roast marshmallows by the fire and tell scary stories?
- Does your family have songs, rhymes, or sayings that get repeated often?
- Do you have a special way of saying good-bye when you drop your kids at school?

I recently heard Caroline Kennedy Schlossberg talk about the special way she and her brother celebrated their parents' birthdays. They each chose a poem to recite from memory. Although she recalls their grumbling about it at the time, as an adult each poem now evokes a special memory.

Family rituals and traditions can be anything you want them to be. They're your very own way of celebrating your bond and strengthening the comfort zone your children live in.

PART 3

■

Lend Support Without Hovering

22. Don't Be a Helicopter Parent

A mother once said to me, "My son doesn't have a care in the world. I do enough worrying for the both of us." Whether your child is a toddler or an adolescent, it is natural to want to help out when he's in a difficult spot. But often we're so intent on keeping our children from experiencing the consequences of neglecting chores, forgetting an assignment, or being irresponsible that we hover over them like helicopters, ready to rescue them at the first sign of trouble. It's so tempting for parents to do for kids what they can do for themselves.

When we do, it relieves our anxiety temporarily, but in the long run, it doesn't make kids stronger or more self-sufficient. Learning to stand back when you're itching to jump in can require enormous self-control, but it may be the ultimate form of generosity and love.

So before you rush to your child's aid, stop and take a moment to ask yourself, "Do I really need to do anything? What will happen if I *don't* remind him to bring home his history book?" Sometimes what your child really needs is benign neglect, as defined by the following do's and don'ts.

■ **Parent's Story: The Overprotective Mother**

When Jody's mother learned that her neighbor's daughter had been making fun of Jody, she was so incensed that she was about to pick up the phone to call her neighbor and tell her a thing or two. Fortunately, the other parents in her parenting workshop dissuaded her, knowing that it was better to try to let the girls work this out between themselves.

Sometimes our own memories of the hurt and rejection we suffered when we were young cause us to want to step in and shield our children from similar pain. These memories may cause us to go beyond just empathizing. But we need to realize that young people are very fickle and less apt to hold on to grudges. The girl who calls your daughter a geek today may be the very one she's sharing secrets with tomorrow.

Don'ts of Teaching Independence

Sometimes what we parents don't do is just as important as what we do:

- **Don't offer to intervene** too quickly before giving your child a chance to work things out on his own. Solving a child's problem for him might make *you* feel better, but when you empower your child to figure out solutions for himself, *he* feels better. Besides, you can always provide help later if he really does need it.

- **Don't get bogged down in imagining the what-ifs.** Accept the fact that life is uncertain. There are always going to be things you can't control.

- **Don't jump to conclusions.** For example, if your child tells you that the teacher kept her back from recess, don't say, "I'm sure you must have done something to deserve it." Instead of assuming the child is at fault or blaming the teacher, listen to your child's explanation first without comment, then ask her what she thinks she can or should do to remedy the situation.

• **Don't tell your child that it's silly to feel upset when he has a problem.** We don't help kids cope by dismissing their strong emotions. It's better to teach that uncomfortable feelings are normal and OK. If you can accept your children's feelings, they'll feel it's safe to come to you when they're upset.

• **Don't push your child to handle problems that are beyond her ability.** Teaching independence doesn't mean forcing your child to cope with situations that frighten her. Avoid saying things like, "You're a big girl. You shouldn't be scared" or "Seven-year-olds should be able to take care of themselves on the school bus." Respect your child's individual pace and abilities.

Do's of Teaching Independence

You can foster independence by putting the following principles into practice:

• **Do let consequences teach.** Resist the urge to nag, remind, and lecture. You might have to accept your child's taking a fall or making a mistake, but it's part of growing up. Most of us learned much more from consequences than from all the warnings our parents bombarded us with.

• **Do offer guidance** rather than solutions when your child complains of a problem. Ask questions such as, "What would you like to say to that person?" or "What can you do the next time this happens?"

- **Do be empathetic.** Let your child know that it's OK to feel sad, angry, scared, disappointed, or frustrated and that you understand those feelings. But fight the instinct to kiss away the hurt and make your child feel better. Of course it's painful for parents to see their children unhappy. But it's often more compassionate to listen nonjudgmentally than to intervene automatically to protect them.

23. Allow Privacy— Up to a Point

Concerned, loving parents who have the best interests of their children at heart are often confused about where to draw the line when it comes to their kids' privacy. Though 99 percent of the parents in a recent national survey said they trust their kids, more than one-third of them admitted to snooping in their rooms or listening in on phone calls.

Here are some answers to the most difficult questions I'm being asked by parents about their kids' privacy.

Is It Ever Acceptable to Snoop in My Kids' Rooms?

If your children haven't given you reason to suspect problems that could affect their health or well-being, leave their diaries, computers, and personal effects alone.

By the time most children are ten years old, they feel strongly about the sanctity of their rooms. Kids need to have a private space where they can play, create, and daydream without fear of parents barging in, uninvited. Generally, parents appreciate their children's need for a private space. But sometimes the urge to snoop can be irresistible. I call invading a child's privacy out of excessive curiosity "unhealthy prying." Even though the temptation may be great to take a peek inside a child's mind and life, acting on such temptation demonstrates a lack of fundamental respect for your child's autonomy. And imagine how you'd feel if the situation were reversed—if you found your son or daughter going through your drawers or personal papers without permission.

How Much Should I Check on My Child?

The majority of parents acknowledge the need to respect their children's privacy, but they also know they must take responsibility for their children's well-being. Sometimes these needs conflict, and it's not easy to know when to intervene.

Don't play the interrogator, especially the minute your child comes home from school. She'll probably tell you more if you give her some space and avoid playing twenty questions. In addition, if you want to have a better idea of what your child does when she's away from home, ask concrete, not general, questions. For example, instead of "How was your day?" ask, "What did they serve for lunch today?"

How Can I Be Sure My Child Is Not Using Drugs?

Parents know that drugs are out there and that even children from loving families can fall into their snare. And we know that kids are being exposed to alcohol and drugs at younger and younger ages.

Some parents who aren't sure about their children's habits buy home drug-testing kits, just to be on the safe side. While it's important to be alert to the dangers to which children may be exposed, parents do more harm than good by insisting their kids be tested if there is no reason to believe they are taking drugs.

Trust is the glue that holds families together, and children might legitimately feel alienated and angry when parents assume they aren't trustworthy. A more positive alternative is to talk with your children about drugs. Try to be as informed as they are—or think they are. Listen to your instincts, and be alert to signs that kids may be experimenting with drugs. It is necessary to be vigilant and not naive. Many parents have found that a zero-tolerance policy won't necessarily keep kids from experimenting. In some cases it may even backfire. However, taking this stand on drugs and underage drinking makes your values on these issues very clear to your child. You know your child, so you need to be alert. Watch for signs of change—in personality, grades, and energy. Be familiar with your child's friends and the people he's spending time with.

Are There Times When My Child Should Lose His Right to Privacy?

Most parents would like to nip serious problems in the bud before they have to launch an all-out privacy invasion. But children also must do their part to earn their parents' trust. This often becomes an issue, especially with preteens and teens.

Trust has to be a two-way street. If children want you to respect their privacy, they owe it to you not to lie when you ask them direct questions about important health or safety matters.

When you take a stand about an issue like smoking, be prepared to be unpopular with your children. Kids are rarely appreciative when parents restrict pleasurable activities or set limits on behavior.

■ **Parent's Story: The Smoking Gun**

"When I was doing laundry, I found a crumpled pack of cigarettes in the pocket of my twelve-year-old daughter's jeans. I asked her for an explanation, and she said that the cigarettes weren't hers. She denied smoking and told me a friend had put them there.

"I wasn't sure if she was telling the truth or not, but I wanted to trust her, and I gave her the benefit of the doubt. Then, a few days later, I smelled cigarette smoke in her room. I went through her drawers and found cigarettes and matches. When I confronted her, she was defensive and enraged that I had gone through her drawers. I felt that she had lost her right to privacy by lying to me about smoking. She strongly disagreed, but this was an issue that was very important, and I stood my ground. I told her that trust has to be a two-way street."

How Can I Get My Child to Talk to Me So That I Don't Have to Pry?

Most parents would prefer not to invade their children's privacy. What they want is for their kids to level with them. Many parents tell me they want to be their child's best friend and confidant—*especially* during their preteen and teen years. That is an unrealistic goal since it is a natural part of adolescence to learn to separate from parents and create an individual identity apart from them. Most kids feel far more comfortable confiding in their peers.

However, if you suspect a problem, talk to your children and listen to them without interrupting or saying too much. Be sure to wait until you are calm and in control. Stress that your concern is for their well-being. Let them know you're on their side and that you're available to be a sounding board to help them make important decisions. Emphasize that you trust them to do what's right and you have faith they will make choices based on their own needs and feelings, not to satisfy someone else who is putting pressure on them.

I remember an occasion when one of my sons came to me with a problem and asked me what he should do. I suppressed my very strong desire to inundate him with my great advice. Instead, I threw the question right back at him: "What do *you* think you should do?" He talked nonstop for twenty minutes. I mostly nodded and listened quietly (not easy or typical for me!). When he was finished, he said, "Thanks, Mom. You were very helpful." I realized that by listening and allowing him to talk, I had been a better "adviser" than if I'd jumped in with my well-meaning opinions.

The best way to avoid privacy conflicts altogether is to establish an environment of trust and open communication early in a child's life. When children learn to see you as their ally and advocate, not as their enemy, they will be more likely to come to you with their real concerns, instead of hiding them from you.

24. Empower Your Children with Choices

When my children were young, I'm sure at times I sounded just like a dictator. The most frequent words out of my mouth were orders. Then one day my son, Todd, then seven, brought me up short by saying, "When you give me an order, I want to do just the opposite." Now that he's an adult (and a delightful, well-functioning one at that), he has his own version, which he reminded me of recently: "When you have a suggestion or advice

■ **Choice Tips**

- **The younger the child, the fewer the choices.** Take care not to offer open-ended choices.
- **Distinguish between a choice and a threat.** For example, saying, "Turn off the TV this minute, or you'll lose your TV rights" is not offering a choice. A choice is saying, "If you turn off the TV now, there will be time for your favorite game before bed."
- **Don't offer a choice when there's really no choice.** Some situations are inflexible. If your child has to go to school soon, there's no point in asking, "Do you want to get dressed for school now?" She probably won't want to, and you will have placed yourself in the unenviable—and impossible—position of having to veto her choice.

and you tell me once, I'll consider it. But when you tell me twice or more, I'm more likely to reject it."

As a result of Todd's remark at age seven, I worked to change my approach. I tried to enforce the rules I considered essential, while allowing my children greater latitude in areas that meant less to me.

The goal of giving choices is to help children feel as if they too have some power and that their preferences matter. In exchange, you gain more cooperation than if you simply bark orders.

If you look at most rules, you can find several different ways of achieving the desired end. Giving your child the option of deciding how the goal is to be reached allows her to feel more in control—and she'll be less likely to resist. If the rule is that she must bathe daily but she fights and stalls all the way into the tub, give her the option of substituting a shower or a sponge bath. If he rejects the delicious pasta you're serving, he can either help himself to yogurt or spread peanut butter on a slice of bread.

25. Be Your Child's Advocate at School

You should be your child's advocate at school, but that does *not* mean hovering, fretting, interfering, and complaining. It does *not* mean behaving like a mother bear protecting her cubs from the dangerous world outside. The best way to be your child's advocate is to establish a cooperative relationship with his teacher, the school administrators, and your fellow parents. While it's natural to be protective of your child's interests—and sometimes that means being assertive—try to start from the premise that you share the same goals.

The following suggestions will help you be a truly effective advocate for your child:

- **Introduce yourself.** At the start of the school year, make it a point to introduce yourself to the teacher and offer your support. Ask the teacher what he or she expects of parents and how you can be most helpful.

- **Be reachable.** Make sure the school office knows how to contact you at all times, especially if there's an emergency. Also be sure to have instructions in writing for your child's special needs.

- **Get involved.** Find out about school activities, and determine how involved you can be. If both parents work outside the home during the day, your involvement in weekday activities is going to be limited. However, you might be able to volunteer for school fairs, attend evening meetings, or participate in special events.

• **Take parent-teacher conferences seriously.** Show respect for the teacher and the importance of the conference by showing up on time and listening to what the teacher has to say. Be prepared with questions—and try not to be defensive if the teacher has anything but glowing remarks to make about your child. It also helps to take notes. This way, if your child is not present, you'll be able to report the teacher's comments to your child more clearly and objectively later. Consider the option of having your child present at the conference. Naturally, you need the school's or teacher's OK; however, I believe there are definite advantages. Instead of talking about your child with the teacher and then coming home and telling her what the teacher said, having your daughter at the meeting empowers her to become part of the process and realize that she, not you, must take responsibility for her behavior and academic performance in class.

• **Play by the rules.** A school is a community that depends on cooperation and compliance with the rules. You can cooperate by making sure your child is on time, dressed appropriately, and prepared. Be fair. If you establish an adversarial relationship with your child's teacher, nobody wins. I've heard too many teachers say that the only time they hear from certain parents is when there's a complaint. If your child says that her teacher has been unfair, don't immediately jump to your child's defense without more information. Instead, try to help your child figure out a solution on her own.

When you let your child's teacher know that you and she share the same goals and that you are acting as a partner not an adversary, your child will be the beneficiary of the ensuing goodwill.

26. Raise a Problem Solver

In today's complicated world, children and adolescents face a greater array of challenges than children did even a generation ago. Simply teaching them to obey their parents—the way many of us were raised—isn't enough to prepare them for life in the real world. A child who is only taught obedience learns how to please other people but may not learn how to develop a system of values, resist peer pressure, handle conflict, or stand up for what he or she believes is right.

What our children really need are problem-solving skills—creative and intelligent ways of responding to choices and conflicts. Here's how to give them direction.

Ask What-If Questions

Myrna Shure, author of *Raising a Thinking Child* (Henry Holt, 1994), devised the "what-if" technique more than a decade ago to defuse playground conflict among young children in inner-city schools. Her books are excellent resources for helping children become more solution-oriented and better at resolving conflict. So, when your child comes to you with a problem or complaint, instead of telling him what to do, ask him to think through the following questions:

- How did you react?
- What else could you have done?
- What happened when you told him that?

The first question helps the child be aware of his responses. The second question helps him to realize there is a wide range of responses from which to choose. The third is a way to make him aware of consequences and outcomes.

Example: You ask your four-year-old, "What can you do if another kid grabs your toy?" He might reply, "I can hit him." Then, instead of saying, "Hitting isn't nice," ask, "What would happen if you hit him?" He might say, "He would hit me back" or "I would get in trouble."

You can turn this exercise into a game, using everyday situations that your kids are likely to encounter. Don't criticize your children's responses—or be too quick to provide answers. Helping children figure things out on their own will add to their feelings of self-confidence.

Create Perspective

Another important aspect of problem solving is considering other points of view. You can help your kids do this by asking them questions about what other people might be feeling or thinking:

- Why do you suppose Grandma worries when you jump on the bed?
- Why do you suppose that kid is always picking on younger kids?

This technique helps children develop empathy, judgment, and perspective—valuable interpersonal skills they will be able to use throughout their lives.

It's tempting when there's a problem to just tell your child what to do. But by doing so you allow her no opportunity to figure out what to do for herself or even to see herself as a capable, responsible person. One mom tried a different approach when her daughter Emma got a last-minute invitation to a friend's birthday party. There was no time to get a gift. Mom couldn't get to the mall, since the baby was sleeping and she didn't want to wake him from his nap. She invited Emma to think about what could be done.

Mom: "Honey, we have a dilemma. Your friend's party is at three, and we have no time to buy her a present. Let's think about how to handle this. Any ideas?"

After exploring various possibilities, Emma came up with one she felt comfortable with.

Emma: "Mom, what if I give her a card promising we'll all go together to pick out a present over the weekend?"
Mom: "Sweetie, I'm proud of you for figuring out what to do. That was a very creative solution."

Encouraging your child to explore options and evaluate the plusses and minuses helps her to think for herself instead of depending on you.

27. Avoid the Homework Trap

Some teachers encourage a great deal of parental involvement, while others want parents to maintain a hands-off attitude. Even within the same school, there may be little unanimity among the faculty.

No wonder well-meaning parents struggle so hard to balance the need to show that they care about their children's academic life with the need to encourage their children to take responsibility for their own work.

I believe that homework should be mainly between your child and his or her teacher. The purpose of homework is to help your child establish independent study habits and to test what she does and does not understand about her work. When you correct misspellings and check papers for every error, the teacher won't see which of your child's skills needs strengthening. Worse yet, homework sessions can easily deteriorate into nightly power struggles that leave both you and your child frustrated and angry. I know a parent is overinvolved when she says, "*We* had so much homework last night."

Letting your child be responsible for his work does not mean showing a lack of interest in what he is learning in school. You can, however, show your interest without getting directly involved in his assignments, by regularly asking questions about his work. For example, ask your son what his book report was about, or say that you would like to hear him read aloud a chapter of a book that he's reading at school. This is not a session in which you critique his efforts. It is simply an opportunity for you to catch up on what he's learning.

One parent told me how she'd gotten out of the trap of fighting with her kid every night to oversee his work. She now leaves it between her son and his teacher and says, "Mrs. S. didn't give *me* any homework—she gave it to you and your classmates."

■ Parent's Story: Hands Off!

"Homework had become such a big hassle between me and my son, Jason, that I'd get a knot in my stomach every night," one mother told me. "Then Jason started misplacing his assignment book or leaving his science book at school. So I'd drive him to other children's houses to borrow books or make copies of homework sheets. I began to see that my overinvolvement wasn't working—and it was exhausting for me. But I didn't reach the end of my rope until one night when I sat up coloring the cover of his social studies report—while he slept!"

This example is not uncommon. On the contrary, over the years I have heard countless stories about the daily battles that occur over homework.

You Know It's Time to Step In When . . .

- **Frustration interferes with learning.** If your child is genuinely stumped by an assignment and is so angry or upset that he can't complete it, you need to help him regain equilibrium. Perhaps you can deliver a snack and some companionship while he takes a time-out from his work. Other times, you may want to suggest that he take the assignment to school unfinished and get individual attention from the teacher during the school day.

- **Procrastination may derail a project.** If the due date for a science project is four days away and your child hasn't even started, you need to help get him back on course. Assist him in breaking a big project into smaller parts.

- **Your child isn't turning in her homework.** Schedule a three-way meeting involving parents, teacher, and child. Your child's presence is crucial so that she can contribute her ideas to develop a homework plan that suits everyone's needs.

- **Your child is having difficulty learning.** Children with a different learning style may need a different approach to homework, as well as supervision. If you suspect that your child has a learning disability, speak with the school psychologist or your family doctor about having him evaluated.

■ **Parent's Story: More or Less**

A mother recalled how she tried to micromanage her son's homework. She wasn't at all successful. He was resistant and resentful of her interference. Her realization: "The more I worried, the less he did."

---

28. Help Your Child Organize for Success

My friend Barbara Hemphill is an organizing expert and author of the *Taming the Paper Tiger* series (Kiplinger Books, 1992). Barbara is a firm believer that taking an organized approach to daily tasks can substantially reduce the stresses of daily life. And believe it or not, even kids can organize for success. Her suggestions are simple to execute and remarkably effective. Not only will your days be less chaotic, but organizing skills can give your child a real sense of control and independence.

Here are a few of my favorite suggestions:

- **Use colors to organize.** If you have more than one child, chances are they spend a lot of time engaged in "It's mine! No, it's *mine!*" battles. The easiest way to solve this problem is to assign each child his own color, then color code everything, from notebooks to bedspreads to toy boxes. Sew color-coded labels in clothing, and use colored stickers on toys and books.

- **Enable with labels.** Help your kids put everything in its place (so it's easy to find when they need it) by clearly labeling drawers, shelves, and bins. For example, if a regular refrain in the mornings is "Mom, I can't find my shoes!" designate a place for shoes, preferably near the front door.

- **Make lists.** Everyone in the family can participate in making lists and checking off items. Keep a running shopping list, posted with a magnet on the refrigerator. If your kids fix their own lunches for school, keep a list of items that are available, such as leftover chicken, apples, and peanut butter cookies. You can even post a wish list. If your child wants a special toy, tell him to put it on the wish list for consideration on the next birthday or Christmas. Adults can participate in the wish list, too. A new book, a night out, or a sweater that caught your eye might show up under the Christmas tree for you.

- **Display a calendar.** Keep track of everyone's schedule with a big, easy-to-read calendar. Barbara suggests that pens or markers with colored ink be attached, so items can be written in each person's color. That way, a quick glance will tell you that Jim has soccer practice and Bob has a music lesson. Parents have told me that an erasable message board is another essential for busy families, especially as kids get older.

Most of us aren't born with innate organizing ability. I wish I had a dollar for the number of times I say, "Where did I put it?" But it's never too late or too early to practice techniques that make for less stress and greater control over the innumerable activities in our daily lives.

29. Separate Without Anxiety

Most young children suffer from separation anxiety at one point or another. They don't have the emotional development or the memory skills to see that a night out for Daddy and Mommy is just a temporary absence. If you work outside the home and your mornings include dropping off your toddler or preschooler at nursery school or day care, you probably experience an extra element of distress and guilt when your toddler turns on the faucets

---

■ **Humor Break**

The comedian Jerry Lewis tells about the time his daughter, then three, was begging him to stay home one evening and not go to the theater where he was performing.

"Daddy, can't you stay home tonight?" she pleaded.

"No, sweetie," he replied. "I have to work, so you can eat."

"But, Daddy," she cried, "I'm not hungry."

---

and cries in a heartrending voice, "Mommy, don't go!" Elizabeth Crary of the Parenting Press in Seattle has a series of children's problem-solving books to read with your little one. One of the most helpful is called *Mommy, Don't Go* (Parenting Press, 1996).

Here are some tips for reducing separation anxiety:

- **Keep the good-byes short.** The best way to handle your good-bye is to keep it short. Not only does this approach reduce the fussing, it sends your child the message that everything is OK.

- **Create a ritual.** You can ease the transition with a regular ritual. One mom I know blows a kiss into her son's palm before she leaves him at nursery school each day. It can help to give your child a transitional object, such as a stuffed animal. When Madeline's three-year-old son became tearful, she pulled off her hair band and slid it over his wrist. "This is your power bracelet," she said. "Wear it until I return." He was delighted, and the power bracelet became part of their daily ritual.

- **Always say good-bye.** Don't try to sneak out without your child seeing you, even if she's playing happily and hasn't noticed you're about to go. When she *does* realize you're gone, she'll be even more upset. Instead, tell her, "Mommy will be back after naptime."

- **Don't ask permission to leave.** There are going to be days when your child just doesn't want to let you go. On those occasions, you might be tempted to delay your leave-taking until you can coax a smile. But most of the time, this will only prolong the agony. Never ask for permission by saying, "Is it OK if Mommy goes to work now?" The answer is bound to be a resounding "No!" Instead, say in a matter-of-fact way, "'Bye now, pumpkin, I'll see you right after snack time."

- **Keep your perspective.** Remember, this too shall pass. The mother of an adult son was complaining one day that he rarely found time to call. "Mind you," she said, "this is the same boy who used to hang onto my leg for dear life every time I left the room. I kind of miss it."

■ **Parent's Story: The Wedding Picture**

Judy's four-year-old daughter, Nikki, was having a difficult time adjusting to her new preschool: "One day when I picked her up, Nikki told me she had been crying at school. She said she didn't know what was making her sad—she'd just start crying. For the next few days, we had long talks about how she'd be OK once she got to know the kids and was used to the school.

"Then one day I picked her up, and Nikki was smiling. She told me she hadn't cried even once that day. I asked her why. I wanted to know which of my words of wisdom had penetrated. She started rustling around in her knapsack and pulled out our eight-by-ten wedding picture, frame and all, which she'd taken from the bureau. She told me that whenever she missed me, she would take out the picture and look at our faces, and she didn't feel sad anymore."

PART 4

■

Show Love Without Spoiling

30. Cure the "Gimmes"

Although nobody wants a greedy, insatiable, overly demanding child, I often get the impression that parents don't really know how to stop this kind of behavior. The way to cure the "gimmes" is to know the difference between what our kids *need* and what they *want*. In this acquisitive, competitive culture, it's often hard for parents to tell the difference. The following guidelines can help you make the distinction clearer for your own children.

Establish Your Values Early On

Start distinguishing wants from needs right away. Once you get into the habit of giving your children everything they want—or everything you think they would want if they could talk—it's harder to stop later on.

Even before a child is fully verbal, he can indicate his desires quite convincingly, by pointing, whining, and grabbing. If you give him most of what he reaches for, he'll come to expect it, and you'll find it more of an effort to resist his pleas in the future—especially if he tends to have a meltdown when you refuse to get him what he's begging for.

When it comes to material things, such as your child wanting a shiny helium balloon he sees at the grocery store or begging you for a cookie, the most effective strategy is consistency. Make it a point not to buy toys or junk food at the supermarket, saying, "We're here to buy groceries." Set limits on when and how often your child is allowed to have a treat. Before you even set foot in the store, remind your child of what to expect.

One mom in my workshop has a wise policy for shopping for birthday presents. Before going into a toy store with her son to purchase a gift for a friend's birthday party, she reminds him, "Jonathan, we're *only* going to get a present for Jeremy. Then we're out of there. Just so you know."

Saying no doesn't have to be a rejection of a request. Often, it can merely be a delay in gratification. For example, you might say, "We'll put that doll on your wish list." These small incidents, taken together, will teach a child that she can't always have what she wants the instant she wants it.

Be a Role Model

Children are very good at picking up cues from your behavior, so be aware of what they observe you saying and doing. Are you displaying a need for immediate gratification in your own life? If your kids see that Dad buys the latest computer gadget the day it hits the stores or hear Mom remark that she just *has* to have that state-of-the-art bread machine, they will likely behave the same way the next time *they* want a new toy. Rather, try to establish values that are less focused on material things. That doesn't necessarily mean you need to be in a constant state of denial. Just be conscious of making the point that you can wait. For example, you might say, "Maybe for my birthday somebody will get that new computer program for me." Don't spend every weekend at the mall acquiring stuff.

When possible, try to de-emphasize the buying frenzy. Encourage your children to think of special ways they can acknowledge a birthday or holiday without making a purchase. Suggest breakfast in bed for Mom on her birthday, or a funny poem or skit for Dad on Father's Day.

■ **On-the-Spot Responses to Halt the Gimmes**
- "Maybe next time. Not today."
- "I'll think about it and get back to you later."
- "Why don't you put that on your wish list?"
- "Oh, you're right. That is an amazing robot. I don't blame you for wanting it."
- "Why don't you save up your allowance so you can buy it?"
- "This *no* will not turn into a *yes*."

31. Beware of Praise That Backfires

How easily the words fly off our tongues when our children are doing well. We love to express delight: "Good girl!" "You're the greatest!" "You're always so thoughtful!" We assume that every such declaration will boost our child's self-esteem and make him more eager to perform well.

Since we mean so well, it's surprising to learn that our words of praise can actually be discouraging or threatening. How is this possible? If you listen to the way adults usually praise children, you'll notice that there's often a judgmental undercurrent:

- **"You ate all your beans. What a good boy!"** This statement tells your child that eating all his beans makes him a good boy. Therefore, if he doesn't eat all his beans, is he a bad boy?

- **"I was so proud when you hit that home run today."** The message is that your pride is reserved for outstanding achievements. If he had not hit a home run, would you still have a reason to be proud of him?

- **"What a smart girl you are! Your teacher says you're the best math student in the third grade."** The implication (by both parent and teacher) is that she has to be the best in the class to earn the admiration of her parents and teacher. If she can't figure out the math problems next week, will they think she wasn't really smart? Perhaps they'll be disappointed and think less of her.

In each of these examples, the adult is offering judgmental praise rather than descriptive praise. Judgmental praise places the focus on the adult being pleased, proud, or full of admiration for a child who has met his parents' expectations of success. Descriptive praise places the focus on the child's efforts and his feelings of accomplishment:

"You ate all your beans! You must have been hungry."
"How did it feel to hit the game-winning home run?"
"Can you show me how you figured out that difficult math problem?"

Children develop high self-esteem when they are made to understand that your love is not based on what grades they get, what they look like, or how many friends they have. Our kids' sense of self-worth grows from the satisfaction they feel from their efforts—even if they don't produce the results they (or you) expect.

Don't Overdo It

As destructive as judgmental praise is, false praise is even worse. Kids can sense when the accolades are genuine and when they're

Parent's Story: Turn Off the Gush Machine

A mother in one of my groups described watching her five-year-old's dance recital. When it was over, her daughter came bouncing over to her, calling, "Did you see me? Was I good?" The mother gushed, "You should be on Broadway! It was the best performance I've ever seen." The girl eyed her mother suspiciously. "You're just saying that because you're my mom. But how did I *really* do?"

nothing more than platitudes. If a parent says to a child just learning to skate, "You're such a great ice-skater, you should be in the Olympics," the child recognizes the statement as overblown. She knows she is not good enough to be in the Olympics. She can hear the lie, and it tends to make her doubt herself instead of providing encouragement.

When Kids Only Aim to Please, They May Stop Taking Risks

Sometimes parents fall into the trap of thinking that heaping on praise can condition their children to behave well and that the more they praise, the more motivated their children will be to excel. But using praise to motivate can be manipulative—and kids sense it. When we place the focus on such external rewards (even verbal ones), we encourage our children to be motivated by the reward, not by their own interests, efforts, or intrinsic sense of accomplishment.

The irony is, when we use praise to motivate our children, they often become dependent on our responses. Once they figure out what pleases us, they tend to play it safe and not take chances or try difficult tasks. Moreover, if a child's attention is always straying from his endeavors to see how he's doing in our eyes, he'll lack the motivation to take risks or try something new.

One parent told me her son was becoming a "praise junkie," always asking, "Are you proud of me, Mommy?"

A father may think he's motivating his daughter to win her tennis tournament by saying, "You can win if you concentrate during your match." But what he's really saying is that if she wins, he will be pleased and proud (as if it were *his* victory), and if she loses, he will be disappointed or even ashamed (as if it were *his* loss). As long as Dad "owns" his daughter's achievements, she can never feel the intrinsic pleasure of doing something she loves just for herself or feel the deep satisfaction of working hard and striving to improve her skills.

The best way to motivate kids is not with words of praise about the outcome but rather with words of encouragement about the process. When we're too result-oriented, we don't teach our children to feel proud of their efforts or inspire them to keep trying.

Children cherish words of encouragement that are nonjudgmental, supportive of their individuality, and most of all, honest. They take great pleasure and pride in describing their accomplishments and moments of glory. And when they are encouraged to experience the incomparable satisfaction that comes from within, words of praise are just icing on the cake.

32. Don't Bribe for Good Behavior

What follows is a typical bribery scenario between a mother and her four-year-old daughter:

Mom: Eat your peas.

Becky: I hate peas!

Mom: Yes, but they're good for you.

Becky: Ugh . . . they're gross and mushy.

Mom: I'll tell you what. If you'll eat just three big bites of peas, I'll give you an extra cookie for dessert.

Becky: Two bites. And I want *two* extra cookies.

Mom: OK, OK, two bites.

Becky: Little ones.

Mom: *(giving up)* OK, but just this once.

The problem with bribery is that it communicates loud and clear, "OK, I give up. I can't make you do what's right. So, what's it worth to you?" It often works to get immediate results in the short run, but in the long run, it can backfire in some fairly significant ways.

Once it becomes a pattern, kids are naturally going to *expect* a payback for doing what you ask. You lose the authoritative voice that says, "I expect you to take my words seriously." And ultimately kids learn that there's a trade-off for appropriate behavior. They don't learn to behave because it makes them feel good or because they respect your authority. They do the right thing only because they want a reward for behaving as they're supposed to anyway.

Bribery Encourages Kids to Be Manipulative

What's the best way to motivate children to brush their teeth, clean their rooms, do their homework, turn off the TV when you ask, and do their chores? In most instances, a parent's own authority is enough. Kids are reassured by our clear, reasonable expectations. However, once you've established a pattern of bribing, it's

---

■   **Parent's Story: A Deal Breaker**

Getting five-year-old Ben to brush his teeth was a nightly problem for his mother. He'd procrastinate and argue, and she would nag and yell. Finally, Mom made a deal: If Ben brushed his teeth thoroughly without making a fuss, at the end of each day he would get fifty cents. It worked great for about two weeks. But one night after Mom said, "OK, time to brush your teeth," Ben replied, "Nah, I don't feel like it."

"But what about our deal?" asked his mother.

"I don't care," Ben said. "Just don't pay me today."

---

very hard to break. But it can be done, as Ellen found with her six-year-old son, Matt:

> **Ellen:** Matt, it's time to put your toys away and throw your dirty clothes in the hamper.
>
> **Matt:** What will you give me if I do?
>
> **Ellen:** *(matter-of-factly)* The satisfaction of a clean room and being able to find your stuff easily.
>
> **Matt:** Last time I cleaned up, you gave me a model car.
>
> **Ellen:** I bet you'd love it if you got a new toy every time you did something I asked. But we're talking about cleaning up here, not a new toy.
>
> **Matt:** I won't do it unless I get a new toy car. That's what you did before.
>
> **Ellen:** I guess you were lucky last time. However, the family rule is, everyone takes care of his own room. Maybe while you're straightening up, you'll be able to find a game we could play together as soon as you're done.

Ellen *did* offer Matt something to look forward to. But she avoided phrasing her request in a way that suggested a bribe: "If you do this, I'll give you that."

Encourage your child to brush his teeth by saying, "After you brush your teeth, it will be time for a story." Such language makes it clear that personal hygiene isn't optional. It also takes the focus off the less pleasant activity, giving your child something fun to look forward to.

Use Rewards . . . but with Caution

When your child does go out of her way for another person, studies hard for a test, or makes a special effort to help you, let her know that you noticed and are proud of her. In these cases, spontaneous rewards are fine. But how are they different from bribes?

A bribe is an offer you make *before* the act: "If you get an A on your language arts test, I'll buy you a new video game." A reward, on the other hand, happens after the fact. It's something a child has earned: "You must be so proud of yourself for getting an A on your math test. This calls for a celebration."

In the end, words of encouragement, expressions of admiration, and appreciation for effort are still the best motivators. Sentiments that come from the heart with no price tag attached can make a child feel ten feet tall. She will then want to do well because it helps her to feel good about herself.

Instead of a Bribe, Give a Direction

Here are some examples of the difference between bribes and directions.

> **Bribe:** "If you dry the dishes, I'll give you money to buy a comic."
> **Direction:** "The dishes need drying. I need your help."

> **Bribe:** If you pick up your clothes, I'll make it worth your while."

Direction: "Clothes don't belong on the floor. Please pick them up now."

Bribe: "If you promise to obey the baby-sitter, I'll bring you a special treat."

Direction: "I expect you to be helpful to Angie while I'm out."

33. Turn Your No into a Yes

"You always say no!" Does this complaint sound familiar? When I admitted to other parents that my initial response to my sons' requests was usually negative, many of them admitted they shared that tendency. If you often respond to your kids' requests by automatically denying them, try a small experiment: keep count of the number of times you say no in a day. This exercise can be enormously enlightening (and somewhat embarrassing). If you accentuate the negative, you've probably discovered that your children often stop taking no for an answer. Instead, they'll keep trying to get you to say yes—so that even if you don't give in, you've always got a battle on your hands.

Sheryl, a mother in one of my workshops, mentioned one day that she was "seriously bugged" by her six-year-old son's habit of pleading for her to buy him a toy or a treat whenever they went to the supermarket. Even though she always said no and usually became upset, Paul just kept on cajoling. "How can I convince him I'm serious so that he'll stop begging?" she asked. "I've run out of ways to say no."

"Maybe you should try saying yes," I suggested. "When Paul asks you to buy him a special treat, you might say something like, 'OK, you can get a treat when we go to the fair on Saturday,' or, 'Sure. Your birthday is coming up, and I'm planning something special.'" Sheryl tried to give up her automatic no, which had usually been followed by a mini-lecture. While it didn't work every time, it did cut down markedly on Paul's whining, as well as making *her* feel less cranky. The strategy works because using positive words instead of negative ones will counter your child's perception that you always say no and never give him anything he wants.

To reduce the number of times you say no while remaining firm, rephrase the same messages in a positive way: "Yes, you can have a cookie—after dinner." "Yes, you can watch TV, as soon as your homework is done." "Yes, you can wear lipstick at home, just not at school." By showing your child that she can get what she wants by following your rules, you're much more likely to earn her cooperation.

What can you do if, having already said no, you realize that you could have just as easily granted your child's wish? You don't want to sound like a wimp by seesawing between yes and no. One way to concede is to say, "You know, Rebecca, staying home instead of going to the park right now isn't a bad idea. I'd never thought of that. If it's important to you, we could leave later." In other words, you're still in charge, but you're taking your daughter's request seriously.

Of course, some noes can't be turned into yeses. When your child asks you for something that you and he both know won't be allowed, simply say, "I'll bet you know the answer to that one!"

34. Don't Be a Pushover Parent

It is rare for a parent to tell me that he or she worries about being too strict. But when it comes to concerns about being too lenient, the floodgates open. Often, I find that parents are filled with self-doubt about when and how to exert authority. They don't want to be constantly nagging their children about their behavior, but neither do they want their homes to be free-for-alls. The question is how to strike a balance.

I think there is a consensus that parents today *are* less strict than previous generations were and children are less obedient. We can't ignore the fact that we live in a more open, permissive society. But that doesn't necessarily mean that we are less effective as parents. What previous generations labeled respect for authority was often just fear, and today most parents have rejected that method of child raising. We don't want our children to be afraid of us—and nowadays most of them aren't. I remember a parent in one of my workshops who talked about the fact that she was proud her kids were totally open with her, since she herself had been much too scared to talk openly with her parents. However, we all laughed when she added somewhat ruefully, "I have to admit, though, there are times when I wish they *were* a little more scared of me."

Trust Your Gut

When my sons were young, I discovered that I had a much easier time enforcing a rule when I believed in it so thoroughly that I didn't care whether they liked it or not. One such rule was nap or quiet time. I knew that if I didn't have an hour of peace every afternoon, I wouldn't be fit to live with. I would make the Wicked Witch of the West look like an angel. The boys seemed to sense that I wasn't going to bend on that rule. They didn't even *try* to argue.

On the other hand, there were rules that I didn't care so much about, and my children could sense that, too. One example was daily baths. Every evening I'd say, "Time to get in the tub," but if they made a fuss, sometimes I'd just let them skip it. The truth was, daily baths weren't high on my list of priorities.

My own experience taught me that it was impossible to set limits when I was even the least bit ambivalent about them. I began to figure out where I could be more flexible, and eventually I came to realize that there were times when it was OK to be less rigid. I found that my children were more cooperative about abiding by hard-and-fast rules when they saw that I was able to be somewhat lenient in other matters. When my kids saw that I was seriously thinking about my answer, they seemed more willing to accept it when the answer was no.

Five Signs That You're Wishy-Washy

Do you worry that your parenting style is too wishy-washy? If the following scenes sound familiar, you may need to reexamine what is getting in the way of your being authoritative:

1. You tell your five-year-old you want him in bed with the lights out by 8:00 P.M. every night. But he usually protests so much that it's at least 9:00 by the time he gets into bed. You always end up being angry at him (and at yourself, too!).
2. Your children are fighting over the TV, and you get mad and tell them that there will be no TV for three days. However, you relent after one day because they're driving you crazy.
3. You're at the store, and your daughter starts whining and begging for a lollipop at the checkout counter. It's against your rule, and she knows it, but you give in because you're too tired to argue and worried that she'll make a scene.
4. You don't approve of your son playing violent war games on his computer. But when he complains that he's the only one in his class who isn't allowed to play the latest game and accuses you of being mean, you feel sorry for him and give in.

5. Before you let your child go on a play date, you want to find out who will be in charge and whether the kids will be watching unsupervised TV, but you're too embarrassed to ask the parent or caregiver, so you let it go.

35. End the Entitlement Mentality

These days when I give talks to parent groups, one question comes up all the time: Why are kids today so demanding? The perception is that our children are never satisfied. They want more of everything—more toys, games, junk food, computer stuff, TV—you name it. At a recent lecture, a man in the audience expressed the feelings of many parents, stating, "Kids today seem to feel entitled to every new toy they see advertised on TV. When I was growing up, it was just understood that my parents weren't going to buy toys and treats for us, except on special occasions. If you wanted it, you waited for your birthday or Christmas. If you were lucky, you'd get one or two gifts. How did we get to this point?"

It's a provocative question. When I ask parents why they think kids today have such a sense of entitlement, they usually talk about our materialistic society, the collapse of cultural values, the influence of TV, and the power of Madison Avenue appealing to every facet of our kids' acquisitiveness. No doubt all of this is true. But they're often taken aback when I suggest a source much closer to home.

A sense of entitlement doesn't just happen. Kids don't acquire it merely by breathing the cultural air. It's not only something they pick up from television or from their friends. It begins at home. Kids feel entitled because parents have given them the mantle of entitlement.

I've noticed an interesting phenomenon. Long before children buy into the idea that they can't live without material things, some parents have already become convinced that it's their job to gratify their child's every wish. For example, a new mother gleefully described to me how she stood in line for an hour to purchase her one-year-old daughter a Teletubby—at the time, the hot new doll for toddlers, inspired by the British television show. "I was so lucky," she said with relief. "I got one of the last dolls left."

"I hope your daughter appreciates your having gone to so much trouble," I said, a bit tongue-in-cheek.

She laughed. "Well, of course she's too young to actually know about Teletubby dolls. But they're so popular, I didn't want her to be without one."

I suspect that parents like this one, though they mean well, have succumbed to a kind of adult peer pressure. They think their kids should be part of the latest fad because everybody else is. Maybe they're afraid of their children feeling left out. Or perhaps the item is something *they* would have liked to have had when they were young. A father in one of my groups described how he'd always longed for a big Lego set when he was little, but his parents couldn't afford it. His three-year-old son is now the owner of a roomful of Legos that he rarely touches.

Before you get swept up in the hype, do a little honest self-examination. Ask yourself, "Does my child really need this? What will happen if I just say no? Why am I so eager to buy it for him?"

The next time you find yourself thinking that your child is entitled to the latest fad or new toy, remind yourself about the things your child *is* entitled to: your love, support, and wisdom to say no.

36. Don't Be Pressured to Play

When my son Eric was five, he used to bore me to tears with his Matchbox cars. Not only did he love those cars, he also loved me to be a part of his games, which consisted of my listening to him describe each car in endless detail—what it could do, where it belonged in his little garage, and so on. I pretended to be interested because I didn't want to hurt his feelings. And I felt I should share in the activity that my son was so passionate about.

But one day, sitting on the floor watching Eric zoom his cars around the room, I unconsciously let out a sigh. He stopped what he was doing and stared at me with a mixture of astonishment and accusation. "You're not interested in my cars?" he asked, as though he couldn't fathom such a thing. The cat was out of the bag, and I felt a twinge of guilt. "It's true," I admitted. "You and your friends have a much better time playing cars than I do."

Parents Aren't Always the Best Playmates

Many parents, looking for that elusive concept called "quality time," assume that they have to grit their teeth and play the games their kids want to play, whenever they possibly can. Although play can be a wonderful way to share our children's world, we needn't feel guilty because they love Barbie dolls and we don't. It isn't our main job as parents to be professional entertainers or ever-eager playmates. Keep in mind, too, that when you're bored, exhausted, or distracted by other concerns, you're not the best playmate anyway.

Engage Kids in Activities *You* Enjoy

When your child asks, "Will you play with me?" and you're not up for another round of Candy Land, you might try introducing him to an activity *you* like. After I revealed my true feelings to Eric about his toy cars, I said, "You know what I would love to do with you instead? Let's make egg salad together." Eric was happy to join me in the kitchen and liked peeling the eggs and mashing them almost as much as he did lining up his cars.

What Kids Really Want Is Time with You

Part of the secret is understanding that what kids really want is not necessarily to play dolls or cars but to spend time with you. As long as your child senses that you're enjoying the time together, it often doesn't matter what you do. This doesn't mean that you should never play the games your child likes. But you can set some limits.

Sarah, a parent who works full-time outside the home, came to dread the moment when she walked in the front door. "As soon as my four-year-old, Amy, saw me, she'd say, 'Let's go into my room, Mommy. I want to play princess!' Feeling guilty that I'd spent the whole day away from her, I'd sit through an agonizingly boring pretend game in which she was the princess and I was everyone else. She would dictate word for word what I was to say, and if I failed to respond on cue, Amy would scold, 'Mommy, you're not paying attention!'

"I finally realized that this routine wasn't working for either of us. I told her, 'Let's schedule a half hour, two days a week, when we play princess, and mark it on our calendar. Then Mommy can be ready. We can schedule other fun activities on the other days—like fixing a special dinner or walking to the park.' Amy was excited by this idea, and we drew a big, colorful calendar, with our 'Princess days' marked, along with our alternative activities." Sarah also avoided the perils of open-ended play dates and the cries of "Mommy, I'm not done!" when it was time to stop. She set a timer for thirty minutes, and Amy was able to accept this clear limit.

When You Do Surrender, Have Fun!

Sarah discovered that once she got into Amy's game and knew she wouldn't be doing it every day, she found herself having more fun. "I started wearing a costume or a hat and ad-libbing a little by saying things in funny accents. And instead of being impatient with my daughter's careful instructions, I became impressed with her attention to detail—down to the inflection she wanted me to use—when she would say things like, 'No, Mommy, do an evil laugh, not a funny laugh.' Maybe she'll be a director some day."

Sarah's observations reflect what many parents have discovered by playing with their children: We learn more about how our children think and what their unique talents are. And we appreciate once again their simple ability to have fun.

One final piece of advice: Find some time to initiate play yourself. You don't want your child to feel that he's always begging you to play. If you periodically say, "Hey, let's play a game," you reinforce the important idea that you genuinely enjoy spending time with your child.

37. Avoid the Happiness Trap

Many parents spoil their kids because they have a hard time saying no. Without knowing it, well-meaning moms and dads fall into what I call the "happiness trap." They simply can't bear to see their children sad or disappointed in any way, so they give them everything they ask or plead for.

Here are five basic strategies for avoiding the happiness trap.

Make Sure *No* Means No

When you say no, does it sound more like *maybe*? If you're at all ambivalent, kids immediately pick up on it. They recognize the signs that you don't want to make them unhappy. They sense it when you're uncomfortable saying no to them. When you don't send a clear message, you encourage pleading, whining, wheedling, arguing, and even tantrums. Remember, although *you're* busy, kids aren't. They will take as much time and effort as they can to get you to change your mind.

Expect your kids to test you. That's their way of finding out whether you really mean what you say. When you have to say no, act secure about doing it. One father I know firmly states, "This *no* will not turn into a *yes*."

Recognize Manipulation, and Don't Give In to It

Be aware of whether you've established patterns with your children that allow them to manipulate you. For example, if your child knows that a public tantrum will make you waver, he's going to find tantrums irresistible. Make it clear that this will no longer work. If you're in a public place, say, "Stop now, or we'll have to leave"—then *do* it. If you're home, say, "Please go to your room until you've calmed down," or just, "I'm sorry you're upset, but I'm not going to change my mind."

Don't Be Afraid of Negative Feelings

One of the sure signs that you've fallen into the happiness trap is that you can't stand to see your children expressing unhappiness or complaining. Let your child know that it is acceptable to feel and express negative emotions. It's helpful to acknowledge her feelings, but let her know that you're going to stick to your decision. For example, instead of saying, "There's no reason to cry," you might say, "I know how much you were looking forward to going to the amusement park. Of course you're disappointed. But I can't let you go while you have a cold."

Focus on Needs, Not Wants

Kids are not always able to distinguish between what they want and what they need. Parents have to do it for them, even if it makes their children momentarily unhappy. Unfortunately, too many moms and dads are confused themselves about the difference. You only have to look at all the parents who line up for hours before Christmas to buy their child the newest hard-to-get toy. Kids are conditioned to want everything they see, and when they want something, they want it with their whole being: "Dad, I've *got* to have that game." "But, Mom, you know I've wanted a kitten all my life!"

Of course, denying children their desires can feel uncomfortable. Don't expect them to give you a big hug and say, "Oh, thank you, Mom, for not buying me that skateboard."

But disappointed children are not unloved children. Also, realize that a child isn't necessarily happier when he does get whatever he wants. In fact, children feel much more secure when there are clear boundaries.

Just because your child expresses a desire, it doesn't mean you have to respond with an immediate yes or no. Sometimes it's more effective to say, "Let me think about it and get back to you later." And do get back to him. Sometimes you will be surprised to find that by the time you're ready to discuss it, your child won't be as interested anymore.

Be a Parent, Not a Friend

Sometimes parents who grew up in strict households want their kids to be raised in more open and flexible environments. There's nothing wrong with that. The problem arises when you try to be your child's friend rather than his parent.

For example, you refuse to let your child go biking after school because you think he's too young to be out unsupervised. He's furious with you and yells, "I hate you!" This kind of statement can really hurt or anger a parent—especially if you're not clear that your role is to sometimes be unpopular with your kids.

Instead of feeling guilty or caving in, you might say, "I'm sorry you feel that way, and I can see you're mad—but the answer is still no."

No parent deliberately falls into the happiness trap. Usually, the parent is motivated by intense feelings of love and caring. The happiness trap becomes easier to avoid when we learn to get rid of our own guilt, recognize the difference between needs and wants, and believe that the happiest child is the one who is given both love and limits.

PART 5

■

Open Communication Channels

38. Listen with Empathy

Julie's eight-year-old daughter, Susan, was having a hard time adjusting to her new glasses. It didn't help that some of her schoolmates continued to tease her. The first time Susan came home from school crying because the children had taunted her and called her Four Eyes, Julie's heart went out to her daughter. She hated seeing her hurt. "They don't know what they're talking about," she said soothingly. "You look adorable in glasses. Just ignore them."

To Julie's frustration, her reassurances didn't seem to make Susan feel any better. And the taunts from her classmates continued. After a few days of this, Julie was once again trying to convince Susan that whatever those girls said was not worth getting upset about, when her daughter yelled, "You just don't understand," and ran from the room.

Julie was stunned. "At first, I couldn't figure out why she was so angry," says Julie. "I thought I was being helpful. But then I realized she was right. I wasn't really listening to her hurt feelings. I was only trying to make them go away."

A while later, Julie went to her daughter's room and sat down on the bed.

Julie: Boy, I guess it's a rotten feeling to be teased and called Four Eyes.
Susan: Yeah. If I cry, they get even worse.

Julie: I know. When I was about your age, whenever my big brothers teased me, crying made them even meaner. I wonder what you could say the next time that would work better.

For the next half hour, Julie and Susan came up with a strategy. "It was hard at first," Julie admits. "What I really wanted to do was build a protective bubble around my daughter so that no one could hurt her. But the only thing that helped was acknowledging Susan's hurt feelings and helping her to figure out how to stand up for herself."

Listening with empathy lets your children know you're on their side. The process of responding empathically is an acquired skill. Unless it was a familiar part of our own upbringing, it's not something that comes naturally. However, it's one of the most important skills we can acquire. People of all ages—not just kids—feel loved when they feel we understand them. And from a child's perspective, there's nothing better.

39. Don't Overexplain

The parents I meet often feel very strongly about communicating with their children on a deeper level than just spewing directives. Many of them recall their own childhoods as being full of rigid rules and endless orders, which seemed arbitrary and inconsiderate of their feelings. They believe that children are *entitled* to explanations and think that if they don't at least *try* to talk things through, they're not treating their child with respect. They also hate being too abrupt; it can feel so unkind or impatient.

Many parents who reason excessively have trouble saying no. They're looking for something to cushion the disappointment, and they think explanations are it. The truth is, when you get into the habit of endlessly explaining every decision, it only makes your child more inclined to argue. And some issues are nonnegotiable: you wear a seat belt because that's the law; you hold hands crossing the street because that's the rule.

Parents also have the belief (I think it's a fantasy) that if they give their child enough reasons, he will happily change his mind about what he wanted in the first place. What they think of as reasoning, however, is really an attempt at convincing. Consider this dialogue my student Mary had with her five-year-old, Isobel, who didn't want to be left home with a sitter while her parents went out to dinner:

> **Isobel:** I want to go, too!
> **Mom:** You don't really want to go. You and Sandy always have so much fun when she baby-sits.
> **Isobel:** I want to go with you. I don't want Sandy to come.
> **Mom:** You told me you were looking forward to being with Sandy. She's your favorite baby-sitter.
> **Isobel:** I don't care. I want to go with you.
> **Mom:** But, sweetie, you'd be so bored sitting in that fancy restaurant.
> **Isobel:** No, I wouldn't!
> **Mom:** Besides, the food is yucky. They don't even cook the fish, and you hate rice. Raw fish and rice! Ick!
> **Isobel:** I could take just a little bite. Maybe I'd like it.

It's not hard to see where this conversation was heading. Clearly, Isobel had one thing on her mind and one thing only: she wanted to go with her parents. And try as she might, her mother was not going to convince Isobel that she really wanted to stay home. Instead, Mary needed to cut the discussion short with some loving words and a firm good-bye:

> **Mom:** Come and give me a big hug, Isobel. We're leaving.
> **Isobel:** I want to come!
> **Mom:** *(hugging Isobel)* I know, honey. We'll go out together one night soon. But tonight Daddy and I are having a grown-up play date.
> **Isobel:** Why can't I come?
> **Mom:** Maybe some other time, but we have to go now.
> *(Kissing Isobel, she gets up and leaves.)*

Here's a tip: if by the time your child reaches the age of five, you're starting to feel as if he is ready for law school or could qualify for the school debating team, that's a sure signal to reason less and state your case firmly and clearly without endless explanations.

40. Make Time for Your Kids

Time has become our most precious commodity. There's never enough of it. I often see parents coming into my workshops almost breathless, as if they've just been running a marathon. In a sense they *have*. Modern life has left most people feeling like they have too much to do and too little time in which to do it. So much stress revolves around time—the lack of it and the pressures connected with this too-limited commodity.

If you feel so overwhelmed by the "musts" and "shoulds" of your life that you never have enough time to enjoy your children, here are some ideas from parents I know.

Decide What's Important

People are always saying, "If only I weren't so busy," without really examining how to slow down and build in more time to spend with their children. Time management is certainly helpful, but it involves much more than rearranging the items on your "to do" list. Maybe your list is just too long. It's hard to give up the entrenched belief that busyness in itself is a virtue. You may find ways to spend time and to save time—but for what? The key to managing your time better is to reevaluate what really matters and relinquish some of the shoulds that may be cluttering up your days.

Strategy: Try making a list of everything you do in the course of a day. Next, divide your list items into three categories: musts, shoulds, and pleasures. For example, paying the bills is a must, but vacuuming the living room may be a should. Under pleasures, you might list reading a book or taking your child biking. After you review the categories, try to think of ways you can cut down on the shoulds, organize the musts, and increase the pleasures.

■ Parent's Story: Pay Attention!

"The other morning, as I was dropping my kids off at school, my oldest was looking at the car in front of us, where another mother was doing the same thing. This mom was talking on her cell phone. She hardly stopped the car while her kids were getting out. As she pulled away, the two of them stood there waving. She was still talking on the phone and never looked back. If you could have seen the look on those kids' faces, it would have broken your heart. We are all in such a hurry these days, and our kids are paying the price. They must sometimes feel as if they are nothing more than an errand to be done."

Practice Family Sharing

The best way to make your children feel important and included in your life is to involve them in the activity of being a family. Many parents separate the ordinary tasks of the day from the "quality time" they spend with their kids. However, most children (especially when they're young) enjoy being a part of Mom and Dad's daily activities. Kids often feel proud and important when they are given the chance to be useful.

Strategy: Involve your children in your own activities. If you're cooking, let your child help peel carrots. When you're doing laundry, ask her to separate the lights from the darks or match socks. When you're working in the garden, show her how to plant a seed. The tasks may take a little longer and require more of your patience, but the time will be well spent in building a bond between you and your child. This kind of involvement also helps your child feel like a valued member of the family, sending the message that what she does makes a difference and she can be relied upon to make a contribution.

Take Off Your Work Hat at Home

Although it's not always possible, try to separate your work life from your home life. Kids become discouraged if they wait eagerly for Mom or Dad to arrive home from a full day at the office, only to have them disappear from view to continue working throughout the evening. Or parents may become so preoccupied with what happened at work that they can't be emotionally present to the kids.

Strategies: One mother I know finishes her extra work on the train coming home, then shuts her briefcase for the night. She makes it a rule not to open it again until she gets back on the train in the morning. One father solved the problem by giving time to be with his kids priority treatment on his daily calendar. He schedules family time on his calendar at work, just as he does sales meetings and conferences. His secretary reminds him of his family as well as his work appointments: "You have a baseball date with John at two o'clock." A mom who is the CEO of a major company sets aside every Wednesday for early dinner at five-thirty.

Have One-on-One Time

Children cherish special times alone with each parent. I have often heard stories from adults who still remember fondly the way "Dad and I used to shoot baskets for a half an hour after dinner" or "Mom and I played duets on the piano." These memories are cherished because they recall times when a parent was totally in the moment and solely focused on being with his or her child, one on one.

Strategy: When you're really squeezed for time, try to find ways to carve out several moments with your kids. A mother in my workshop makes it a point to take a fifteen-minute walk with her seven-year-old daughter every evening after dinner, weather permitting. Another parent has a ten-minute evening ritual in which she asks her preschooler, "Tell me about the best part of your day." An artist I know gives his son a twenty-minute drawing lesson every night. Together, they choose their favorites to send to relatives. And almost every parent I know has a goodnight ritual at bedtime.

It's easy to tell a child, "I love you," but it's the actual time that we spend fully focused on her alone that makes her feel important and worthwhile.

I've never yet heard a parent of grown kids say they wish they'd spent more time at the office when their children were young.

The events of September 11th brought this home to us more poignantly than anything ever has before. This tragedy made us aware of what matters most: to put family first and to validate the important people in our lives.

41. Avoid Red-Flag Words

Red-flag words are those simple expressions that almost always escalate any conflict with a child as well as a spouse or anyone with whom we have a close relationship. By becoming aware of common words that backfire, we can substitute expressions that are more likely to result in cooperation and understanding.

Most red-flag words or phrases occur at or near the beginning of a sentence. Here are some alternatives to two seemingly innocuous words that are among the worst offenders: *if* and *why*.

"If You . . . "

If—usually followed by *you*—sends up a red flag when used as a threat:

> "If you don't put your toys away, I'm giving them all to the Salvation Army."
> "If you can't take care of your clothes, I'm not buying any for the rest of the year."

Many children perceive a threat as a challenge and may repeat the offense just to test the parent's resolve. Worse, these threats are often impossible to carry out. And if we don't follow through on the threat, our child stops taking us seriously.

In addition, a threat that is irrational or out of proportion to the offense doesn't teach the child anything about the realistic consequences of her behavior.

Better Choice: Instead of *if*, use *as soon as* or *when*. These phrases are more positive and less punitive. They encourage you to stay rational and to make a realistic statement that you can then follow through on:

> "As soon as you put your toys away, we'll have a snack."
> "When you've hung up your jacket, we can play a game."

"Why Don't/Can't/Won't You . . . "

Why also sends up a red flag, especially when followed by *don't you, can't you,* or *won't you*:

> "Why don't you ever pick up your things?"
> "Why can't you keep your hands to yourself?"
> "Why won't you listen?"

These questions are unanswerable. In fact, we're not asking why because we expect a rational answer. Instead, we are really just blaming or making a critical statement. Children are not likely to cooperate when they feel they are being accused.

Another common use of the word *why* is in "Why did you . . . ," as in, "Why did you hit your sister?" Most children don't even know why they do what they do. They're basically impulsive and spontaneous creatures.

Better Choice: Leave out that useless word *why*, and change the question to a clear, firm, nonaccusatory statement:

> "Those toys need to be picked up."
> "There will be no hitting."

"I would appreciate your hanging up your jacket without my reminding you."

At worst, these are global statements about a child's character, which he can't change, as opposed to statements about his behavior, which he does have some control over. Accusations put people—children and adults alike—on the defensive, and a defensive person is certainly not motivated to change for the better or improve his behavior to please you.

■ **Parent's Story: The Power of Words**

"My bag was stolen. My husband, angry and annoyed, said, 'You're always leaving your things all over the place. If you weren't so careless, it wouldn't have happened.' His words enraged me and made me feel stupid. But that evening, my ten-year-old son heard about the loss. He put his arms around me and said, 'Oh, Ma, you must feel terrible.'"

The moral of the story: When things go wrong, try not to tell your loved ones what's wrong with *them*.

---

42. Open a Dialogue with Your Teen and Preteen

By the time our children are preteens, we're beginning to feel a complicated pull of parental emotions. On one hand, we want our children to become more independent and self-sufficient. On the other hand, we worry about protecting them from the myriad dangers this independence brings.

The key is to keep the lines of communication open. Encourage your preteens and teens to tell you where they're going, who they'll be with, and when they'll be back. They may not like the questioning. Trust is a big issue with preteens and teens. One of their biggest complaints to parents is "You don't trust me." Expect them to use that line—it's their way of trying to convince you to say yes instead of no. You can say, "I trust you, but I don't like the situation. You won't have control over what can happen when you're at friends' homes and there's no adult present." Some parents tell their kids, "I trust you to stay away from trouble, but I can't be sure about the other kids."

You can also ask about safety issues: "Do your friends' parents have a gun in the house?" "Is the liquor locked up?" "Will her parent(s) be at home?" It's also very helpful to keep in close touch with the parents of your kids' friends.

You can't pick your preteen and teen's friends the way you did when they were in preschool or elementary school. But you can help them practice ways to resist negative peer pressure. Give your kids "lines" to use when they are in a tight spot, and rehearse these scenarios with them.

For example, there's a party next weekend. You know parents will be chaperoning, but you also know that some kids stash liquor and drugs outside or in their clothing or purses. Discuss these possibilities ahead of time with your child, and ask what-if questions: "What if your friends dare you to try a joint? Guzzle a beer?" Then give them a way out or suggest excuses they can use: "You can blame me, make me the bad guy. You can say, 'My dad always smells my breath when I come home,' or, 'I'll get grounded for a month if my mom finds out.'"

Also establish a family coming-home ritual. If you'll be asleep when they arrive home, let your kids know you expect them to come in and say good night to you. Like all rituals, this one reminds them that they're expected to check in. It also assures you that they've come home safe and, you hope, sober.

Finally, during your child's early adolescence, accept the fact that you're going to be at your most unpopular. Your child's goal is to push your limits, so be prepared to be inundated by a barrage of complaints and accusations for every rule you establish.

Many parents believe that they have to spend less time with their kids as they get older. When our kids are little, we spend a lot of time on maintenance chores (dressing, feeding, bathing, supervising their activities), so we may assume that kids need less of our time as they get older and more independent. Just the opposite is true. Older kids need as much or more of our time, but it is a different kind of time. Not maintenance, but the ability to listen more than talk and to keep trying to maintain moments of connection.

In *Our Last Best Shot* (Riverhead Books, 2000), Laura Sessions Stepp writes, "Parents who easily demonstrated love when a child was young can be uncertain how to behave once puberty starts. Parents pull away rather than giving a hug in private, a kiss on the head, a squeeze of the arm. This is unfortunate . . . because adolescents crave physical contact even when they seem to be pushing you away."

For example, a mother in my workshop told me of her surprise when her thirteen-year-old said to her—five minutes after telling her mother to leave her alone and get out of her room— "Don't you know when I say go away it means I need you around?" No wonder parents of teens are confused since they get so many mixed messages.

We need to stay constantly available, while at the same time not hovering or being overly intrusive. And even when they reject it or act embarrassed, never hesitate to remind your teenagers of your love.

■ Parent's Story: Breaking the Teen Code

"My fourteen-year-old daughter, Gillian, lives with her father in Connecticut because she attends school out there. She and I were recently on a shopping expedition to buy her bathing suits for our upcoming trip. Before we left our apartment, Gillian asked me if she could go out that night with two boys I had never met. I said, 'I guess so. As long as I know where you're going and you're back by eleven.'

"On our way down the street, Gillian said, 'Mom, I'm really glad you trust me and are so much more lenient about my social life than Dad is.' My first reaction was to feel flattered. Then alarm bells went off. I was forced to rethink my approval of her evening plans, and I told her I had to meet these boys before she went out with them. Gillian got all upset about this. She begged me to stick with my original acceptance of her plans, but I wouldn't budge.

"I sensed she herself was not altogether happy about the evening's prospects and that was the reason she had paid me the seeming compliment about my leniency. She made a huge fuss, but as soon as we got home, she called one of the boys and told him she couldn't go out with them because her mother insisted on their coming over first. Gillian then begged off their plans and began to telephone friends furiously to find substitute arrangements. I realized that deep down she was relieved that I had intervened because her mood started to change and she was all sweetness and light for the rest of the day.

"Ever since then, I listen to her words very carefully and try to figure out what she is truly trying to tell me. They speak in code, you know. And I guess it's our job as parents to try to break it."

43. Acknowledge the Validity of Feelings

Let's face it. It's not so easy to listen to children when they are expressing angry or hurt feelings. It's much easier and more pleasant to listen when they express positive emotions. We all feel cheered when a child comes home from school and exclaims, "Mom, my teacher said I handed in a perfect paper, and she gave me a gold star," or declares delightedly, "The baby is so much fun. She really makes me laugh." It's an entirely different matter when the message isn't so upbeat. When an older child complains constantly about a new sibling, it's tempting to deny his resentment and jealousy.

Many parents mistakenly believe that they should try to talk children out of feeling angry, pessimistic, or sad. Of course we don't want our children to be unhappy, but we don't have the power to make things OK for them all the time. Telling a child who's been rejected for the baseball team, "You'll get over it—it's not the end of the world," denies how hurt he feels. Nor will a toddler whose baby brother just broke his favorite toy be consoled if you tell him, "Don't make such a fuss. He didn't mean it." Comments like these make children feel as if we neither understand nor care how they feel.

It's not really our job to solve our children's dilemmas. Nor is it within our power to make them happy when they're not. But no matter what age our children are, we can communicate to them that their feelings are valid and that they're not in any way bad for having those feelings.

Acknowledging feelings is a crucial skill for parents to master. Here are some specific strategies:

- **Describe** what you hear or see, without making a judgment. For example, your eight-year-old complains that he has too much homework. Don't respond by preaching—"You're in the third grade now. You can't expect school to be all fun and games"—or by denying, contradicting, or criticizing—"Why are you always complaining? That's really an easy assignment." Instead, respond in a descriptive, nonjudgmental way: "It does seem like a lot of work. Third grade isn't easy."

- **Acknowledge** the feeling—what it must be like for the child. For example, your four-year-old says, "It's too dark in here. I'm scared the monsters will come." Try not to respond, "Don't be ridiculous. There's no such thing as monsters," or, "Don't act like a baby," or, "You're just making excuses not to go to bed." To acknowledge the feeling, you might say, "I guess going to sleep in a dark room can be scary. What can we do to make it not so scary?"

- **Repeat or paraphrase** when you're not sure what to say or need more information. For example, your child says, "The bus driver yelled at me in front of all my friends." Avoid saying, "You must have deserved it" or "What did you do now?" These responses presume your child is guilty before you know the facts. Instead, you might say, "He yelled at you in front of all your friends? Wow!" This response will be more likely to elicit further details about what happened.

I always remind parents to be permissive with feelings and strict with behavior. A person can't help what he feels. He *can* help how he behaves. As parents, our job is to help children realize that there's a crucial distinction between words and actions. The message is feel what you feel, but control what you do.

■ **Parent's Story: The Therapeutic Grunt**

Never underestimate the power of a grunt. The therapeutic grunt is simple and powerful. When you murmur sympathetically, it lets your child know you're listening, yet it's completely nonjudgmental. It's also a good way to elicit more information.

One parent told me how she tried the technique with her son Billy. When Billy complained to her that his teacher was unfair, her reply was a simple "Mmmm. . . ." Not feeling threatened, he continued talking. "She's really a dork," he said.

"She's a dork?" she replied.

"Yeah. She said I didn't study, because I gave a wrong answer. But I did study. I just didn't know that one."

"Ummm," said his mother, adding, "You think she wasn't fair. How would you like to handle this? Any idea of what you might say to her?"

44. Keep It Simple

Children tune us out when we talk on and on. Instead of a lecture, keep it short and simple:

"Walk."
"Boots—jacket—bag."
"Hands." (When they need washing.)
"Dishes." (When it's time to put them in the dishwasher.)

A mother of a preteen constantly complained of his fresh, disdainful attitude when she'd ask him to help out or listen. After a few sessions in which we discussed this topic of selective hearing, she reported a major change: "He has been a lot more cooperative lately. He even thanked me the other day for helping him out."

I was impressed. "Are you doing anything differently that might account for this change?"

"Well, Nancy," she said, "the only change I'm aware of is that I say only about one-tenth of what I used to."

Practice Saying Nothing

Pretend you have a bad case of laryngitis and can't speak for a day. What might the consequences be? If you were unable to give constant reminders, instructions, and orders, your children might:

- Leave the house without their coats on
- Make a mess
- Forget to walk the dog
- Fail to brush their teeth
- Lose their hats and mittens
- Eat a cookie before dinner

Now ask yourself, "Would that be so terrible?"

I still remember years ago when I was a teacher. To my surprise, on those rare occasions when I *did* suffer from laryngitis, the kids were amazingly cooperative.

■ **Tip: Count Your Words**

A pediatrician I know counsels parents, "If you are trying to explain something to your toddlers and preschoolers, use as many words as they are years old." What a remedy for talking less!

---

45. Put It in Writing

A written message to your child is a powerful way to raise a difficult issue, make up after a stormy battle, or express love and admiration. I've found writing notes to be one of the most effective communication tools parents can use to strengthen the bond with their children. Here are three situations where putting your thoughts in writing can enable a dialogue.

After an Argument

In every parent-child relationship, there are times when we utter angry, harsh words that we wouldn't use if we were feeling more rational. Once we've calmed down, a written message can go a long way toward soothing hurt feelings and restoring a loving atmosphere.

One mother was furious when she returned from work one day and was told by the baby-sitter that Jack had defied her by refusing to come inside and do his homework when she called him. She confronted Jack angrily and shouted, "If I can't trust you

---

■ **Parent's Story: Words to Cherish**

"When my son, Paul, was six, we got into an angry argument. I can't remember what it was about. I said some hurtful words that I regretted, and later I wrote him a little note, apologizing. That night I found a card from Paul on my dresser. It read, "Dear Mom, Even when I'm mad and sad, I still love you." I was very touched and also amazed that a little boy could express such a profound thought. That was twenty years ago. To this day I've kept that card."

---

to behave responsibly, you can just forget about going on that hiking trip this weekend!" Jack ran crying to his room.

Later, after Mom had calmed down, she wrote a note and slipped it under his door:

Dear Jack,

I was upset that you ignored our rule about doing homework and were rude to Carol, who is responsible for you, but I apologize for yelling. I know it can be hard to leave your friends and come inside, especially on such a beautiful day. But I need to know I can count on you to do the right thing when I'm not here. Let's talk about this now that we've both calmed down. I love you.

Mom

After reading his mother's note, Jack opened the door and came out of his room. "I'm sorry for not coming in when Carol called me," he said. Mom gave him a hug, and Jack promised her it would not happen again.

When You Need to Make a Serious Point

Written messages can help get a point across without excessive arguing and wrangling. For example, Martin's twelve-year-old daughter begged him to let her go to the mall after school with her friends. He said no. She accused him of being unfair. Later he wrote this letter and placed it on her dresser:

Dear Becca,

I know you find it hard to understand why I won't go along with your wishes. You've always been responsible when you go out. However, I don't trust the scene at the mall, so I've decided it's off-limits unless you have an adult with you. This is a safety issue, and it's not open to negotiation. But I welcome your suggestions.

Love,
Dad

Becca didn't comment directly about the message, but that night she slipped a note underneath her parents' bedroom door:

Dear Dad,

Jennifer's mother won't let her go either. Can you take us and try not to be too obvious about it?

Love,
You-know-who

When You Want to Express Love and Admiration

Sometimes we're so busy criticizing our children's faults that we forget to express our love and pride. Writing is a creative way to put our feelings into a tangible record that can endure for a lifetime.

When a friend was in the hospital giving birth to her second child, she wrote to her six-year-old, who had never been separated from her mother before:

Dear Leslie,

It's so lonely here in the hospital without you! I miss the fun we have together, and I can't wait to see you. Daddy and Grandma have told me what a help you've been, and I'm very proud of you. You're the best daughter a mother could have. I'll be home tomorrow with your baby brother, and the first thing I'm going to do is give you a huge hug. Sleep tight. I love you.

Mommy

Her daughter still reads the letter often and keeps it in a special place.

There's another important advantage, which so many parents who write notes and send E-mail have told me over the years. Their kids end up doing the same thing, and they become very comfortable expressing their thoughts, feelings, and requests in writing.

For example, my younger son, Todd, who is now an adult, often prefers communicating with us in writing. Over the years he has sent my husband and me letters that we treasure. These are proof, too, that even with less than stellar parenting skills we can have a relationship with our grown children that is one of love and mutual respect. Thank you, Todd, for giving me permission to include the following letter:

Dear Mom,

This isn't a Mother's Day card. It's a thank-you note. I want to let you know how much I appreciate everything you have done for me, including raising me to care about education, knowledge, health, right and wrong, striving for excellence, and many other things.

You taught me to read and communicate at a level that has given me a distinct advantage over others.

Throughout the years you have listened to my complaints, problems, and gripes with patience and a desire to help me in any way possible. I value your advice and assistance.

I am fortunate to have you and you are fortunate to have me. For us, nothing is more important than family.

Happy Mother's Day!

Your lifelong friend,
Todd

46. Help Your Kids Tell the Truth

Most of the parents I know feel very strongly that their children should always tell the truth. They know that people who are honest inspire trust and confidence. It's an important value. It's also a necessity because parents need to have reliable information, especially when their child's safety is involved. How can you encourage an atmosphere of honesty in your home? Here are some suggestions.

Tell the Truth Yourself

One of the best ways to teach honesty is to set a good example. Children will not respect the truth if they see that there are times when they catch you in a lie. And they are amazingly observant, noticing when your words don't match your actions.

Many adults feel they can justify telling a lie when the situation warrants it. But they don't always see the negative effect that even a fib can have on children. A man I know still remembers how he cringed when his father secured a cheaper bus ticket for him by telling the driver that he was five when he was really six. A friend remembers how her mother used to drive very fast, but whenever she was stopped by a police officer, she always denied that she was speeding.

Try not to lie in front of your children, even when it would be easier to tell a half-truth. For instance, instead of begging off from a social situation by pretending to be sick, simply say, "I don't feel up to it," or, "This isn't a good time for me."

Don't Overreact to Small Lies

Most kids tell small lies to avoid getting punished or incurring a parent's anger. This is normal self-protective behavior.

If you catch your children in a "Yes, I washed my hands" type of lie, resist launching into a tirade. Instead, calmly remind them that the truth is a value in your household and that you expect them to be honest. But don't blow it out of proportion.

Remember to focus on the incident of dishonesty, instead of drawing broad conclusions about your child's personality. Instead of "You're a liar," say, "You didn't tell me the truth about how that cake disappeared from the refrigerator." When parents feel their trust has been violated, they often become angry and risk making children feel that they are habitual liars with serious character flaws.

For example, if your child assures you that he has finished his homework and you later find out he did only part of it, don't make a blanket accusation, such as, "I see I can't trust you." It's better to say, "When I ask you a question, I'm upset if I can't count on you to tell me the whole truth." This approach is more likely to open the door for a fearless and truthful answer.

Don't Punish Honesty

While telling the truth sometimes means facing up to unpleasant consequences, you need to help your child feel safe enough to be able to tell you the truth. For example, when your child does tell you something that he knows might upset or disappoint you, you'll encourage his capacity for honesty by saying, "It means a lot to me that you told me what really happened."

When your child is truthful about something that was difficult for him to admit to, make a point of acknowledging it. That

■ **Parent's Story: The Smoking Game**

Jack, a dad in my workshop, had a vivid recollection from his childhood. His father came into his room, smelled cigarette smoke, and said, "Were you smoking?" to which Jack replied, "If I tell you the truth, will I be punished?" His father said, "Yes, you know you're not supposed to smoke." "OK," said Jack, "then I wasn't smoking."

doesn't mean you have to let him off the hook, but your praise for his honesty or his difficult admission will encourage him to tell the truth in future situations.

If a negative consequence is in order, make sure children understand that the penalty was for violating the rules of the house, not for telling the truth. For example, if your child owns up to losing your cell phone, you might say, "I know it took a lot of courage for you to tell me what you did. I truly appreciate your honesty. However, we need to discuss how you can help pay for a new phone."

Don't Use Entrapment

If we don't want our kids to lie, we have to take care not to entrap them. I call this asking Fifth Amendment questions—you already know the answer, but you ask the question anyway, which encourages a child to lie.

If you see chocolate smeared on your child's face, don't ask, "Did you eat the candy I was saving for company?" If she is like most kids, she'll deny it. Instead of putting her on the defensive, simply state the fact: "That candy was for guests only."

Understand that sometimes it is easier for a child to tell a lie. Helping your child to become truthful is a process that requires your patience and sensitivity.

47. Nix the Nagging

Maryanne, a mother in one of my workshops, had terrible memories of her mother's constant nagging and was determined not to do the same with her daughter. "The more my mother harped on something, the more I dug in my heels. I wanted to teach Alice appropriate behavior without having to repeat everything a hundred times," she recalls. But Alice, a curious two-year-old, wasn't cooperating with the game plan. When she decided she wanted something, she'd go after it, no matter how many times her mother said no. She'd pull all the books out of the bookcase or sneak snacks from the kitchen before dinner. All day long, Maryanne found herself saying, "Leave that alone," or, "Stop it!" to no avail. Eventually, she became so exasperated that her tone grew sharper. "Alice, I've told you a hundred times—no! Why won't you listen to me?"

Deep down, Maryanne knew the answer: because she'd become a nag. Alice was tuning her out the way she'd tuned out her own mother. The problem was, Maryanne didn't know what else to do to get her daughter to listen.

No parent wants to be a nag. So why do so many of us end up that way, and how can we avoid it? The truth is, the only way to stop nagging is to stop talking—and start taking steps to correct the problem. "You can talk until you're blue in the face," a mother in one of my groups said wryly. "You can yell until you're purple. But if you're using that preachy 'mother tone,' you might as well be talking to the wall."

Often we fool ourselves into thinking that our valuable lessons are something other than nagging. We think, "My child won't ever pick up his toys, do his homework, think twice about hurting someone's feelings, keep away from the stove," and so on without endless verbal reminders. Or we worry that important messages about safety or morals or manners won't get through without constant nagging. The problem is that this kind of lecturing rarely works.

One reason that kids respond so negatively to our exasperated reproofs is that they're left feeling humiliated. Before you say anything, imagine how you'd express the same message to a child who was not your own. For example, if a neighbor's child was having dinner at your home, I doubt that you would shout, "Stop wiping your mouth on your sleeve—that's really gross!" Chances are, if you said anything at all, it would be stated in a gentler tone, such as, "Here, let me give you a napkin." Or you might act without any words and simply hand him one. There are many occasions throughout the day when you would do better to simply act and not speak at all: take your child's hand when it's time to leave the playground or give her a sponge when she spills juice on the table.

Most parents spend a lot of time issuing constant reminders. They assume that's what they're supposed to do to impress upon their children the important lessons they need to learn. I believe reminders are just a euphemism for nagging. And kids tune us out faster than we can say, "Don't forget . . . ."

■ Parent's Story: Let the Experts Do the Talking

Cathy's five-year-old son had a fascination with lighting matches. She lectured and nagged to no avail. He still wasn't listening. One day she caught him burning paper in his bedroom, and she was as upset as she had ever been in her life. This time, instead of launching into her usual lecture, she said quietly, "Put your coat on." Then she marched him down the street to the fire station and asked the captain to speak with her son about the dangers of fire. By the end of their talk, this child vowed he'd never light another match, and he didn't.

Can you really blame them? Imagine how you would feel if your boss repeated instructions over and over, in a disdainful, aggravated tone. So what can you do instead? Enforce consequences and take action. That's what Leslie, a mom in one of my workshops, did.

Every evening when she put dinner on the kitchen table, Leslie would call out to her two children in the living room, "Turn off the TV and come to dinner." Two minutes later, the TV would still be on. Leslie would shout, "I said, it's time to turn off the TV and come to dinner."

Usually Leslie had to make at least one more call from the kitchen before the TV would be shut off, or she would have to go and do it herself. I asked Leslie if she had any idea why they were turning a deaf ear to her repeated requests. "I know they're not hearing impaired," she said. "They just ignore me until I totally lose it."

I suggested that she try the speak-once-then-act strategy. The first night, when her kids didn't respond to her first call, Leslie walked into the living room and turned off the television without saying a word. The kids howled in protest, but they did get off the couch and come to dinner. Later she calmly suggested to them that it was inconvenient for her to stop what she was doing and go in to turn the TV off. "It would be easier for me if it were never turned on," she said, then stopped, letting this sink in. The second night, as soon as the children heard her footsteps, they shut off the TV. Within a week, they were turning it off after one call.

In studies of successful marriages, researchers have found that an essential element in a happy marriage is for the loving communications to outweigh the critical ones. The same dynamic holds true with children. When the words our children hear from us usually sound critical, resentful, or peevish instead of helpful, loving, and encouraging, their desire to cooperate and sense of self-worth can plummet.

■ **Parent's Story: Come-On-Hurry-Up**

"My three-year-old thought her full name was Karen Come-On. I started to notice how many times in a day I said, 'Come on, hurry up.' It was embarrassing!"

---

48. Offer Comfort and Wisdom in Troubled Times

The terrorist attacks on the World Trade Center and the Pentagon occurred as I was completing work on this book. The unimaginable scope of this horrific act sent parents reeling. Even those who did not personally know anyone lost in the tragedy were shocked and uncertain about how to address their children's fears. One mother spoke for many when she said, "How can I comfort my children and tell them they're safe when I don't believe it myself? The truth is we're *not* safe. I know it, and my children know it."

Events like this one remind parents that, while our job is to protect our children, sometimes we're at the mercy of circumstances beyond our control. Since the events of 9/11 the world has become a more frightening place, and to varying degrees, we are constantly confronted with our vulnerabilities. Still, we can do much to guide and comfort our children in times of crisis and loss. Many websites give helpful information, including the American Counseling Association and the U.S. Department of Education. Here are some steps parents can take to help their children cope:

1. Give your children different opportunities to express their feelings about what happened, and share your own feelings with them. Regressive behavior (for example, thumb sucking, night waking, and bed-wetting) may occur in response to trauma. Instead of reprimanding your child for this behavior, help him put his feelings into words.

2. Reassure your children that they are loved and that you are working very hard to keep them safe.

3. Be honest about what has occurred, but confine information to what is age-appropriate. Older children usually know when something is being sugarcoated, but younger children may be better off with very limited explanations.

4. Spend extra time with your child, especially doing something fun or relaxing for both of you.

5. Give lots of hugs. Sometimes a hug or a loving touch can reassure children more than words.

6. After any crisis, try to return yourself, your children, and your family to as normal a routine as possible. This helps provide a sense of security and safety.

7. When your community or family encounters acts of hate, violence, or intolerance, take advantage of the opportunity to teach your children a positive lesson about tolerance and understanding. Help them see things from another person's point of view. Avoid negative stereotyping of ethnic, racial, or religious groups.

8. Talk about the senselessness of violence and hate and what it means to live in a caring community.

9. When a disaster strikes, be it a terrorist attack, a natural disaster, or a community crisis, engage your children in activities where they can offer help to victims. Teach them that they are a vital part of the community. For example, young children can send drawings, cards, and caring

messages. Teens can donate blood or volunteer with community organizations.

Are Positive Lessons Possible?

After the terrorist attacks of September 11, 2001, we were all forced to ask ourselves if any good could come from this tragedy. In many ways, this event transformed the everydayness of our lives into the priceless treasure it should always be. It reminded us to live our lives fully every day. That means remembering to tell those you love how much you love them. Hug them and touch them with your words and gestures. Cuddle with your little ones. Try to take advantage of each day to let them know how much you care. Don't forget the most important gift our kids and teens need from us—that of our time. Time to listen without speaking, time to cry together and dry their tears, time to enjoy one another. Children can help us heal, too, if we allow ourselves to share their exuberance and bask in their silliness, giggles, and laughter.

PART 6

Use Positive Discipline

49. Express Anger Without Doing Damage

Parents often feel the most guilt when they fly off the handle or lose their temper with their kids. When they think about the times they've expressed anger—not to mention uncontrollable, purple-faced rage—most parents feel that somehow they've failed. But anger is a normal human emotion, and people tend to get angriest at those they love the most. The issue isn't how to stop the anger. It's what to do when the inevitable rage hits.

Here are some handy escape hatches for when things get out of hand:

- **Take an adult time-out.** When we become so incensed that we're about to lose control, exiting from the scene or calling for a brief time-out can give us a breather so that we're not at the mercy of our words or emotions. And exiting can be a powerful way of showing self-control and demonstrating to your child how serious you think the situation is. As I explain in one of my earlier books, *Love and Anger: The Parental Dilemma*, there are three four-letter words (all ending in the letters *i* and *t*) to act on when anger makes you see red: exit, wait, quit.

    Leave the room, put on earphones, or shut yourself in the bathroom. (If need be, put babies and toddlers in a crib, where you know they'll be safe for a few minutes.) Briefly let your children know why you're leaving the scene. For example, you might say, "I'm feeling so furious right now that I don't want to see you until I've calmed down."

Small children may follow you and they *will* be upset when you walk away. However, the alternative—screaming, hitting, or verbally attacking your child—is more damaging. So, although removing yourself from your child may not be ideal, it's often the lesser of two evils.

- **Hold your tongue.** Angry, hurt, upset people cannot have a civil discussion or reason with one another, so if your child provokes you to the point of anger, try to say nothing for a minute. We are at our most vulnerable and are least able to discipline effectively when we're upset. At those moments, remind yourself, "I will respond more effectively if I calm down first." The wonderful thing about saying nothing is that you never have to take it back. Or as one wise person said, "He who hesitates is probably right."

- **Maintain a perspective.** Sometimes kids will display annoying behavior just to goad you into a reaction. They'll chase each other through the house, trade nasty insults at the dinner table, and wheedle and whine long after you've said no. Before you go to the mat over a particular issue, ask yourself, "Will this matter a week from now?" or, "How important is this?" In the time it takes you to answer that question, you will begin to cool down.

- **Recognize when you're at risk.** What sometimes happens with rage is the "last straw" reaction. Incidents have been piling up and you've been holding it all in—but then one more little thing happens. That's when you can't resist the impulse to list all the annoying things your child has done that day or week or month. But most kids simply tune out after the first accusation or two.

Be aware that the temptation to lash out at your child, verbally or physically, is greatest when you're at your wit's end. Avoid getting in that state by taking care of yourself and taking time out— even if it's only five precious minutes alone in the bathroom.

■ **Parent's Story: When Anger Begets More Anger**

A father in one of my groups told me how incensed he was when he came home from work to find that his son had borrowed his new laptop computer without permission. To make matters worse, when confronted, his son denied he'd taken it, blaming his older sister. Dad became enraged, lost control, and called his son every name in the book, telling him where he'd end up and which loser in the family his son reminded him of. The son, reeling from his father's insults, ran from the room, yelling, "I hate you!" Instead of feeling remorseful or conscience stricken, all the son could feel was rage at his dad.

---

50. Spare the Rod

If there is one discipline method that's sure to inspire heated debate, it's spanking. Indeed, a "spare the rod, spoil the child" mentality seems to be making a comeback. I've even heard some of the parents who participate in my workshops say there's nothing wrong with an occasional spanking to "teach kids respect." Many tell me that the more benign forms of discipline, such as time-outs, don't work, especially with younger children. That may be true, but I believe spanking is rarely, if ever, an effective alternative.

These are the most common rationales I hear and why I don't think they are valid.

"I Spank So That My Child Knows What It Feels Like"

Four-year-old Martin was placing the final block on his castle when his baby sister knocked it over. Martin was furious at her for ruining his creation, so he hit her. Their mother, Joan, who had witnessed the scene, was equally furious at the way he had lashed out. As she spanked Martin, she said, "This will teach you not to hit your little sister! Now you know how it feels!"

"She wrecked my castle!" Martin yelled. "You always take her side. I hate you!"

It's unlikely that Martin felt apologetic after he was spanked. And he certainly was not motivated to get along better with his sister. By spanking Martin, Joan was modeling the very behavior she was trying to prevent, sending him the message that hitting is an acceptable way to solve problems. It's convoluted logic for her to hit her son to teach him *not* to hit his sister.

A more effective solution would be to firmly state, "Hitting is not allowed in this house. I don't blame you for being mad, but I won't let you hurt her." And Joan might suggest that next time she will help him set up a work area that is out of his sister's reach. The key to this approach is consistency. If you establish a non-negotiable rule of no hitting in your family—and abide by it yourself—your children are less likely to use hitting as a way to settle their disputes.

"Sometimes I Just Lose It"

It's a rare parent who doesn't lose control on occasion. Many parents, when they're being totally honest, admit that spanking doesn't usually occur in calm, rational moments. In spite of the difficulty, we have to make a real effort to handle our anger in other ways—after all, we're supposed to be the adults. I'm not proud to admit that when my kids made me really mad, I sometimes descended to their level—and even beyond. Eric was three, and I became two! I still remember the knee-jerk reaction of wanting to shake him, squeeze his arm, or scream in his face.

When you're really enraged, it's best to leave the scene until you can calm down. Chances are, once you've had some time to cool down, you won't feel so inclined to inflict pain.

"I Only Spank to Reinforce Safety Lessons"

Even parents who don't generally spank say that there are exceptions, especially when the issue is safety. Sandra, for example, described how she spanked her seven-year-old daughter, Sue, when she ran out into the middle of the street to chase a ball: "If the driver hadn't slammed on his brakes, Sue could have been killed. This was serious, and I wanted her to know it. Spanking was the only way to impress upon her that she must look both ways before crossing."

But two weeks later, Sandra was telling a different story. "I thought Sue got my message after I spanked her. But a couple of days ago, I let her walk to her friend's house across the street by herself. As I watched her from our window, I saw that *again* she didn't look before crossing. I couldn't believe that she could still be so careless."

I suggested that a better approach might be to rehearse each step with Sue: look right, then left, check the light, and glance around the corner. In the meantime, Sue should not be allowed to cross any street unsupervised until she proves she knows how to be careful.

"I Spank So That My Kids Will Know I Mean Business"

I've frequently heard parents express concern that if they don't occasionally spank, their kids will turn out to be wild or spoiled. They argue that they themselves were spanked as children, and they turned out OK. But being a nonspanker doesn't mean being overly permissive. In fact, spanking is the easy way out—for parent and child alike. Hitting a child lets parents release their anger and feel as though they've addressed the problem. However, when a child is spanked, he tends to feel let off the hook. ("I've been punished, so I don't have to think about it anymore.") He doesn't learn what to do instead. Nor does it help him develop a conscience that makes him feel bad about doing the wrong thing. Rather, kids quickly figure out that the best way to avoid getting hit is to make sure they don't get caught.

When you as a parent develop a nonspanking attitude, you are truly a force to be reckoned with. Your child will understand that you're not going to react to misbehavior with a spanking that's over in a minute. You're going to force him to examine his actions and help him behave differently.

■ Parent's Story: "Bad Boy!"

"I had told my five-year-old many times that my desk was off-limits, so when he got into my desk drawer where I keep my important papers and bills, I slapped him on the hand and told him he was a bad boy. Then, about half an hour later, I saw him out in the yard. Our dog had dug a hole in the garden, and my son was swatting him on the back and shouting, 'Bad dog! Bad dog!' I realized that he had learned from me that when you do the wrong thing, you need to get hit."

Inflicting pain by hitting, slapping, striking, spanking, and punching does not teach children to look for nonviolent solutions to their problems. What really influences children to do well, to be responsible and considerate, and to develop a conscience is the strong bond they establish with their parents, who are their models and teachers. This bond should be one of love, trust, and mutual respect, not one of anger, fear, and pain.

51. Find Alternatives to Blowing Up

Hitting and spanking usually occur in the heat of the moment, when you're angry, scared, or simply up to your eyeballs in frustration and don't know what else to do. But when you're able to be in control of your anger, you'll have far more control over your children. And when you look beyond your reactions of the moment, you *can* find long-term solutions to discipline problems. Here are some effective alternatives to spanking I've learned from the experts—parents themselves.

Make an Impression

A mother in one of my workshops said that she didn't usually believe in spanking but felt it was necessary after her three-year-old was about to stick her finger into an electrical socket. "My heart almost stopped," she said. "I spanked her hard because I was so terrified and I wanted her to know it."

I can understand the compulsion to spank in such a circumstance. However, this mother probably succeeded only in frightening her child and calling more attention to the pain of the spanking than to the wrongdoing itself. Mom might have made her point more forcefully if she had squatted down, looked her daughter in the eye, grasped her shoulders, and stated in a voice that was equal parts fear and fury, "You are *never* to do that again!"

Speak Firmly

Recently, a mother stood up during the question-and-answer period in one of my lectures and said that the only thing that made her children listen was the threat of a spanking. She was taken aback when I suggested that maybe she lacked the voice of authority.

The voice of authority is the most effective discipline tool there is. Most of us remember an adult from our childhood, perhaps a parent, teacher, or coach, who was able to stop us short with a word or even a look. Those adults had true authority because they appealed not to fear but to conscience. They were also consistent in their responses. They said things once, and only once, and followed up with action if necessary. If they announced, "If you can't sit at the table without bickering, we're leaving the restaurant," we knew they meant exactly that. Because they were unwavering, their words carried a lot of weight. I like to call this person "the credible parent."

Hold Them Accountable

One mother described an incident in which her seven-year-old son said a vulgar word in front of her mother-in-law. "I was so embarrassed and horrified that I slapped him," she told me. "I didn't want my mother-in-law to think that I would let him get away with it."

"What happened when you slapped him?" I asked.

She grimaced. "He gave me a look of such pure hatred that it made me shudder. I immediately realized it was the wrong thing to do. He didn't feel bad about being rude; he acted like a victim, full of rage at me. It certainly didn't encourage him to change his rude behavior."

What could this mother have done instead? She might have said very coolly and firmly, "That word is totally unacceptable. As soon as we get home, we're going to talk about this." Later, after a conversation about inappropriate language, she could have had him write his grandmother a note or call her on the phone to apologize, holding him accountable for his actions and teaching him far more than a smack could. It would have been a better way

---

■ Keep Your Cool

- **Your kids' fighting is driving you up the wall.** Don't spank—divide and conquer. Announce, "If you guys can't play nicely together, you need to be apart." Chances are, that's not what they really want. Being sent off alone can be comparable to kid-style Siberia. It can also provide them an opportunity to cool off.

- **Your three-year-old draws on the wallpaper with felt-tip pens.** Take a deep breath and try to put yourself in your tiny artist's shoes. She doesn't understand why you complimented her on her pretty drawing yesterday but are furious today. Explain that drawing is for paper, not the walls, and clean up together. And buy only washable markers!

- **Your four-year-old is rude to one of your friends, telling her she's stupid.** It's embarrassing when children behave disrespectfully toward other adults. Have your child dictate a note of apology or make a phone call and face the music himself.

---

to impress upon him that other people's feelings matter and that being rude or insulting won't be tolerated.

52. Watch Your Mouth

When a child does something to make us angry, our automatic response may be to shout an accusation: "Why are you behaving like such a brat?" "What kind of a slob are you—throwing your jacket on the floor?" "You are impossible!" The message we communicate is that the *child* is unacceptable, not the action.

Parents in my workshops often recall the phrases their parents used with them in times of anger and disappointment. Remembering how wounding those phrases were, they're horrified and ashamed when they hear the same words coming out of their own mouths. Most of us can identify with at least some of these red-flag phrases:

- I'll give you something to cry about.
- Wait till your father gets home.
- It served you right. You got just what you deserved.
- Shame on you.
- Who do you think you are?
- You're driving me to drink.
- Don't you dare!
- You're just like your father (mother).
- Wipe that smile off your face.
- You're so . . . /you're such a . . . (brat, spoiled brat, selfish, slob, ungrateful).
- You'll be the death of me.
- Wait till you have children like yourself. Then you'll be sorry!

These all-too-common expressions of anger and frustration are "you" statements: they either start with the word *you* or imply it by denigrating your child and letting him know how he has let you down. In contrast, you can make the point much more effectively, without damaging a child's self-esteem, by using "I" statements. An "I" statement starts by telling what *you* feel or what *you* observe. When you're angry, it's better to say (or even shout), "I'm mad!" instead of, "You're bad!"

For instance, instead of saying, "What a pig you are, always ruining your nice clothes. Do you think money grows on trees?" you might say, "I am very angry that you tore your new dress." State how *you* feel rather than making a declaration about the child's character: "I need quiet right now," "I am furious that you broke our rule," and "I won't listen when you call me names." All of these are effective "I" statements.

The words and labels we use with our children can sometimes stay with them for life and are often repeated from one generation to the next. We have much better things to pass on to our kids than hurtful phrases.

I try to remind parents of a statement Dr. Alice Ginott often used: "What's on our lungs shouldn't always be on our tongues."

53. Encourage Cooperation with Humor

Mom: Knock, knock.
Chris: Who's there?
Mom: Orange.
Chris: Orange who?
Mom: Orange ya going to set the table for dinner?

Six-year-old Chris's mom, Leslie, appealed to his passion for corny jokes when she wanted him to stop watching TV and set the table. Chris was absolutely delighted. At that moment, the TV couldn't compete with his funny mom. Trying to contain his giggles, he replied:

Chris: Knock, knock.
Mom: Who's there?
Chris: Berry.
Mom: Berry who?
Chris: Berry soon, I'll set the table.

Leslie laughed appreciatively, and Chris jumped up from the couch and went into the kitchen. Mission accomplished—and they were having fun!

Leslie's technique is an inspired alternative to the more common and less effective methods of yelling, ordering, and asking twenty times. Yet the idea of using humor as a tool to elicit cooperation doesn't occur to many parents, because they're so busy being too serious. Besides, when most of your parenting time is spent trying to get your kids to do things they don't want to do, lightheartedness often seems impossible.

Humor can be a very effective parenting tool, precisely because kids are inherently playful and fun oriented. In fact, one of the most appealing things about kids is their sense of fun and playfulness. Is there an adult alive who can resist a smile or a giggle at a three-year-old's silly antics or a toddler's waddle? Humor enables you to discover a lighter perspective on parenting. Sure, there are serious matters that need to be dealt with firmly, but not every occasion requires a stern approach. If you're communicating a sense of humor instead of a sense of "wipe that smile off your face," your children usually will be more willing to go along with you.

Included here are some of my favorite funny-bone strategies from parents.

Be Outrageous

Five-year-old Cynthia and seven-year-old Eric were constantly running to Marcia to get her to settle their petty disputes. One day, she'd had enough.

> **Cynthia:** Mom! He's making funny faces and breathing his stinky breath at me!
>
> **Mom:** *(in a horrified voice)* He's *what*? He's making funny faces and *breathing* on you? Oh, that's awful! I can't believe it. This is an emergency. I'm going to call the police! Quick—let's dial 911.

Even the kids saw the absurdity of this reaction, and they recognized Mom's mock horror. Sometimes when you exaggerate the importance of a complaint, kids see for themselves that it's not such a big deal. In this instance, Cynthia avoided being trapped into taking sides and laughed off the entire incident:

> **Cynthia:** Oh, Mom, you're so silly. We were just playing around.

It's almost impossible for kids to stay mad when they see their parents being silly. Monica, a mother in my workshop, told me that when her son cries, "I hate you!" she replies, "Well, I just looooove you," and chases him around planting wet kisses on him until he's helpless with laughter.

A word of caution: If a child is really angry, sometimes humor can backfire. We need to be very sure that we're laughing *with* our kids and they don't feel as if we're laughing *at* them, making fun

---

■ Parent's Story: Proper Humor

Humor can be an effective way to defuse anger. Four-year-old Richard was very angry at his mom. "You're stupid!" he shouted. Without missing a beat, Mom replied, "I'm *Mrs.* Stupid to you." She *could* have given Richard her ten-minute lecture on how it wasn't nice to call people names, which she'd done countless times in the past. The humorous approach worked much better.

---

of them, or being sarcastic. Back off right away if your humor seems to be making your child more upset.

Reverse Roles

Kids will almost always laugh when you playact being a baby or growl like an animal. And even very young children seem to get the joke when you reverse roles with them. There are three benefits to this technique: one, it's funny; two, it give kids a good idea of what they sound like; and three, it often leads to a level of cooperation that seemed impossible before. In the following example, a weary mom tried a bedtime switch on her daughter Leanne:

> **Leanne:** *(whining)* I don't want to go to bed.
> **Mom:** *(yawning)* I sure do. I'm so tired. I hope you don't mind if I just lie down here in your bed and snuggle in. You can straighten up the house and make the school lunches for tomorrow. *(loud sounds of Mommy snoring)*
> **Leanne:** Hey! Get up! That's my bed.
> **Mom:** Ohhhh, please!
> **Leanne:** *(laughing harder)* Come on, Mommy! Get up! I want to go to bed.

Mom: *(slowly sitting up and stretching)* Oh, all right. It's all warm now. Go ahead. I'll let you take my place.

The challenge to "turn your frown upside down" may sound corny, but it's great advice for harried parents. When you let go of the need to be too earnest, you find a side of yourself that no amount of rule making and rigidity can achieve. Humor is a sure-fire way to bond with your kids. And you see once again what is so magical about being a child—and so delightful about being in a child's presence.

54. Don't Punish—Teach

As any parent knows, one of the most difficult tasks we face is teaching our children to think, reason, plan ahead, and anticipate the results of their actions—in other words, how to be responsible. The best way to accomplish this is by helping our kids learn through consequences.

When I discuss the importance of teaching children about consequences, parents often respond, "Aren't consequences just a fancy way of saying 'punishment'?" In fact, the two are not the same. Punishment is usually ineffective because its aim is to make the child feel bad, not to help him behave differently the next time. Using consequences gives children a way to anticipate the results of unacceptable behavior and to participate in a plan to change that behavior. Think of it as a more advanced version of your telling a toddler, "Hot!" in order to keep her from touching the stove.

One way or another, kids ultimately discover that their behavior has a profound effect on the people around them. And the way children feel about themselves is critical to the way they treat other people. You're far better off making your child part of the solution instead of the problem.

Try these ideas instead of punishment:

- **Tell them clearly, calmly, firmly what to do.** Tell them what you expect. If they argue, don't get trapped in arguing back. Simply use the "broken record" technique. Repeat your statement calmly and firmly: "Homework before TV . . . Coats go in the closet . . . Seat belts."

- **Express strong disapproval, if necessary.** Tell your children how you feel about their behavior and why you feel that way. But be careful not to attack their personality or label them: "This kind of horseplay must stop. Somebody could get hurt badly."

- **Tell or show your child how to take care of the problem.** "I know you didn't mean to spill cereal all over the floor, but I'll show you how to use the dustpan and broom to clean up the mess."

- **Give a choice, but only a choice you can live with.** "You may sit in the stroller or walk beside me, but you have to stay with me."

- **Take action.** When you have given a choice or stated your expectations, follow through: "Since you're not holding my hand, I'm putting you back in the stroller."

Punishment often doesn't decrease the problem behavior. If you continue to punish a child over and over again and the behavior doesn't change, it's time to look for a different approach. Punishments fail when we try to "teach our children a lesson" out of anger or express a knee-jerk reaction that sends the message "now you're going to be sorry." A child who is filled with rage and the desire to get even has learned nothing about changing his behavior. I admire the way Barbara Coloroso, in her inspiring book, *Kids Are Worth It* (Avon Books, 1995), defines discipline: "Discipline is not judgmental, arbitrary, confusing, or coercive . . . Our goal as parents is to give life to our children's learning—to instruct, to teach, to help them develop self-discipline."

55. Inspire Remorse, Not Resentment

One of the goals of positive discipline is to help children be aware of unacceptable behavior and to instill a desire to do better. Yet many of the disciplinary methods parents use don't have this effect at all. Instead, punishment disguised as discipline can make a child feel resentment and fury toward the parent. That's one reason spanking is so ineffective. If we think back to our reactions as children when a parent spanked us, it's doubtful that any of us were remorseful. Nor were we feeling grateful that they cared enough to teach us a lesson. More likely, we were consumed by feelings of helplessness, humiliation, and revenge. (Many of us remember our parents saying when they spanked us, "This hurts me more than it hurts you." We didn't really understand what they meant by that, but it didn't ring true, since we were the ones who were feeling the pain.)

This point was brought home recently in one of my workshops. Beverly, the mother of a five-year-old son, Phillip, was

■ **Parent's Story: The Blame Game**

Angela, age eight, wanted her mother to send away for five favorite things she'd chosen from the Lands' End catalog. Mom said she would once Angela had cleaned her room. Angela procrastinated and delayed for over a week. When she finally finished her room, Mom called to order the items, and only one was still in stock. Angela was furious, and she tried to pin the blame on her mother for waiting too long to order.

When kids get madder at you than at themselves, they no longer have to take responsibility for their own actions. Angela tried to bait her mom by getting her to say, "I warned you," or "It serves you right. If you'd cleaned your room right away, you'd probably have gotten what you wanted." Mom, knowing that these remarks would only have made Angela madder at her than she was at herself, didn't take the bait. Instead, she let her daughter vent and said nothing.

describing a scene from the previous week. Phillip had left his new baseball glove on a park bench, and it had been stolen. "I told Phillip that if he took his glove to the park, he would have to keep it with him at all times," Beverly recalled. "Now he was heartbroken, but I was too furious to feel any sympathy."

Beverly went on to describe how she snapped at Phillip, "You've got no reason to cry. See what happens when you don't take care of your things? You got exactly what you deserved."

"Of course, that only made him cry harder," Beverly said. "I told him to go to his room, and he screamed, 'I hate you!' and ran out of the room. Why did he hate *me*? *I* wasn't the one who lost the glove!"

Maybe not, but Phillip wasn't making that distinction. He wasn't considering the way his own careless actions had such unfortunate consequences. He was only hearing his mother's voice of blame, and all of his fury was directed at her, not at himself.

I could certainly understand why Beverly reacted as she did. But I also wanted her to know the difference between making Phillip suffer for his carelessness and teaching him to be accountable for his possessions. It's the difference between telling your child, "Now you see what happens when you don't listen to me?" and, "I'm very sorry you lost your glove. I know it's going to be hard to be without your glove."

The goal of positive discipline is to help a child reflect on his behavior and work toward change. When he's angrier at his parent than at himself, the opportunity to teach has been lost.

56. Remove Temptation

We were discussing discipline in my workshop group one morning, when Donna, the mother of a two-year-old, spoke up. "I agree that it's probably not appropriate to spank a child once you can reason with him. But my daughter Maggie basically acts on instinct. She's too young to listen to explanations. When she puts filthy toys in her mouth or goes to stick her fingers in the electrical outlet or knocks over the flower vase, swatting her is the only way I can really impress on her that she must not do it."

I've heard similar explanations from parents of very young children. Some of the parents of toddlers who attend my groups admit to using a swat on the rear end or a slap on the hand to keep their children out of trouble. At this age, warnings and time-outs often aren't effective, while spanking usually stops the behavior, at least for that moment. As one frazzled mom helplessly asked, "Have *you* ever tried to reason with an irrational two-year-old?"

She's right. It's simply not effective to tell a toddler he's not allowed to play with the items in the makeup drawer, the power tools in the closet, or the dials on the stove. Why? Because a young child lacks the cognitive skills to understand the consequences of his actions. But spanking doesn't get the message across any better. A child who is too young to reason will not be able to understand the connection between being swatted and not repeating the behavior. I have the same objection to parents who tell me that the way to teach a biting toddler to stop is to bite him back.

With very young children, it's especially important to distinguish between behavior that is deliberate and behavior that is instinctive. Your toddler is going to find a vase full of pretty flowers irresistible and will automatically go to touch it. She will put an interesting object in her mouth because it's the natural way she learns more about it. Maggie is not trying to be naughty. She's just being two! Every toddler is a "touching machine."

Instead of swatting or punishing a child for something she can't help, you need to reduce the number of temptations in her path. Try to put the things you don't want her to touch out of

---

■ **Parent's Story: The Touching Machine**

"My eighteen-month-old was compelled to touch and examine every item he could get his hands on. To my dismay, Shaun finally mastered the ability to open my makeup drawer in the bathroom. Every time he had a chance, he headed for the drawer. I tried everything to get him to stop. I gave him a swat. I shouted 'No!' Nothing worked. Then I finally hit on a solution. I moved my makeup to a place he couldn't get to it. Guess what? Shaun was no longer interested in the bathroom drawer. He promptly forgot about it."

---

reach, and realize that babies and toddlers will put anything and everything into their mouth. Place safety gates in doorways and on stairways, use cabinet locks, cover electrical outlets, and continuously childproof your home. It will make living with very young children a lot less frustrating.

57. Teach That Mad Is Not Bad

It can be very frightening for parents to see their children expressing anger. Many of us were taught that anger was a totally unacceptable emotion, so when our children are angry, our first reaction may be to talk them out of their feelings. Because it is so upsetting to see them lose control, we want to make these feelings go away. Therefore, we tend to deny or minimize their angry outbursts with statements such as, "It's not the end of the world," "You don't really feel that way," "You're making a big fuss over nothing," "In this house we never say 'hate,'" "Nice girls don't act that way," "What's wrong with you? Of course you love your little brother," "You're not really mad; you're just tired."

But everyone—babies, toddlers, teens, adults—experiences intense anger sometimes. It's up to us as parents to acknowledge our children's anger but to also set limits on how they express it. Our goal as parents is to try not to get mad ourselves or to retaliate. Nor should we make the child feel like he is a bad, unacceptable person. At the same time, all physical aggression must be stopped. Kids need us to be in charge.

Observe what your child does when she gets very angry. She may scream or wail at the top of her lungs, hit, kick, pinch, bite, slam the door, curse, yell "I hate you" or "shut up," spit, have a tantrum, sulk, or whine. If a child is allowed to act out her anger without restrictions, she will find the world a frightening place. Try to offer alternative outlets for your child's anger. "No hitting *people*. Here, you can punch these pillows." "No spitting except in the sink. I'll take you to the sink where you can spit all you want." "You don't have to like your sister, but I won't let you hurt her, and I won't let her hurt you."

The best lesson you can teach your child about anger is that feelings are acceptable—then help him find acceptable ways to express those feelings. Here are some ideas for sorting out those options:

Acceptable Expressions of Anger	Unacceptable Expressions of Anger
Crying	Destroying property
Going outside to sulk	Using four-letter words
Punching a pillow	Hitting, kicking, punching, biting
Saying angry words	Name calling
Hitting the "bop bag"	Spitting
Yelling, "I'm mad!"	Taking it out on the dog
Isolating themselves	Hurting themselves
Making an ugly face	
Writing an angry note	
Drawing an angry picture	
Pounding clay	
Growling	

■ **Parent's Story: A Healthy Example of Anger**

"Zack is out of control and freaking out, jumping on furniture, running wildly through the apartment, and yelling at top volume. I send him to his room to take a break so that he can begin to cool down. When I go in after ten minutes, he's ripping up all his precious Pokemon cards."

Mom: What's going on?

Zack: I just have a lot of anger, and I don't know how to get it out.

Mom: I'm happy you can tell me about it, so we can find a way to work it out.

Zack: *(visibly calmer)* I just need to use my arms and legs a lot. Maybe I can wrestle with Dad every day.

Mom: Zack, I'm impressed. That's a great way to get rid of your anger.

58. Restore Good Feelings

If there has been an angry confrontation, it's important to restore good feelings as soon as possible—once everyone has calmed down.

Parents and children want and need good feelings to prevail, even when the battles become fierce. Time and distance heal many wounds, and a simple apology can diminish resentment and pave the way for reconciliation. Some people are afraid to let their children see that they are vulnerable. But it is a good lesson for children to learn. We are all weak sometimes. We make lots of mistakes with our kids, and we all have regrets. However, when we put a human face on the job of parenting and acknowledge our imperfections, it becomes easier to restore good feelings.

How do you go about restoring good feelings? Sometimes a hug and a simple statement like "Mommy loves you" do the job. Other times, especially with older children, a longer conversation is required. And sometimes, when you've been out of control, you must apologize.

Many people in my workshops report that their parents never apologized to them, nor did they ever admit they were wrong. I think some parents worry that such admissions take away their authority. But it's important for us as parents to show respect for our children's feelings by apologizing when we say or do something we regret. In this way we teach our children that everyone can be wrong sometimes, and that it's OK to admit it.

There are many ways to say "I'm sorry":

"Mommy shouldn't have shouted at you. I didn't mean to hurt your feelings."
"We had a hard time today, didn't we? What can I do to make you feel better?"
"I wish I could erase what I just said. I really lost it."
"I was wrong."
"I don't blame you for being upset. Are you ready to kiss and make up?"
"I'm sorry I lost my temper. Can we start over?"

If we can put a human face on the job of being parents, it becomes easier for good feelings to be restored.

When you're tempted to bawl out your child for being thoughtless, rude, careless, or annoying, stop and try to imagine that you were talking to a stranger or someone you hardly knew. Would you speak the same way?

After a talk I gave in Ohio, a mother in the audience came up and told me the following story: "I had asked my daughter to stop running wildly through the house, but she continued to ignore me.

▦ Parent's Story: Garrett's Gift

"As a single parent, I struggle to use positive discipline with my high-energy, passionate nine-year-old son. Life's stresses, my own wounds, and my own passionate nature often get in the way. One afternoon, I called my son repeatedly to come inside. A neighbor was here, and I was angry that my son didn't come when I called him and angrier that he chose to do this in front of the neighbor. In addition, it was a PMS day, so I was furious over the smallest thing.

"When my son came inside and the neighbor had gone, I shouted at my son for his rude behavior, six inches away from his face, and was generally beside myself with anger. I sent him to his room so that I could cool down, and eventually I did. Later that night, feeling very remorseful about being too angry about such a small thing, I talked with him about it, apologized for losing control, and discussed what we could do differently the next time.

"Then, bearing all the weight of my latest failure in parenting, I worriedly asked him, 'When you're a grown-up and a dad, and there are a lot of stresses in your life, and you come home and the kids misbehave, who are you going to look to as a role model?' He calmly replied, 'You.'

" 'Me!' I said, horrified. 'Me! Why me?'

" 'Because,' he said, 'you never stop trying.' "

Suddenly I heard a crunching sound. She had stepped on my brand-new, expensive, tortoise-shell barrette. I was just about to yell at her, telling her how mad I was and asking her why she had ignored me. However, I took one look at her expression and saw how scared and guilty she appeared. So I controlled myself. Instead I said, 'You know, Cara, it's just a *thing* and things can be replaced. It's not like hurting a person. I know it was an accident and you didn't mean to do it.' 'Oh Mommy, I love you,' she said, her eyes filling with tears. 'I'm so sorry. I didn't mean to break it.' "

PART 7

■

Develop Sibling Harmony

59. Prepare for Number Two

Many parents believe that once they go through the experience of having their first child, the rest is fairly predictable. They are ill prepared for the turmoil that often surrounds the arrival of a second child. Nor are they prepared for the reaction of number one to the "blessed event."

What's the best way to help your child welcome a sibling? There's no foolproof method. Sometimes parents do all the recommended things to plan for the new arrival, only to find that their efforts seem to have been in vain. Other parents do little or nothing at all, and the relationship works out quite smoothly.

Here are a few suggestions.

Breaking the News
- Wait to tell your child (particularly a toddler or preschooler) until three or four months before the birth, if you can. Nine (even seven or eight) months is too long a time for a young child to anticipate.
- Don't wait too long. Make sure your child hears the news from you and not from someone else.
- Encourage questions: "How did that baby get in your stomach?" "How does a baby get out?" Answer them in an age-appropriate way.
- Don't tell a child how he will feel: "You're going to love having a baby sister!"

Before the Baby Comes
- Sign up your child for sibling preparation classes, if you can. They're often offered free at the hospital or birthing center. Be sure the class is age appropriate.
- Ask your child to help you pick out a name for the baby.
- Visit a friend who has had a new baby.
- Let your child feel the baby kicking.
- Talk about what it will be like when the baby comes, stressing all the things an older kid can do that a baby can't.
- Show your child her own baby pictures and talk about her first year of life.
- Don't paint too rosy a picture of what a new baby is like. Help the older child realize that a baby takes a long time before she can become a playmate.

Including your child in the process will help her feel special and important. Knowing what to expect will reduce her anxiety. However, don't be surprised if the idea of a sibling doesn't light up her face. It takes time to adjust to no longer being the only one.

On the *Today* show, Katie Couric told me that when her second child was born, she hired a baby nurse for the first few weeks. When the nurse was about to leave, her older child said, "Hey, nurse, you forgot your baby!"

So, be prepared for the unpredictable!

60. Help Your Child Welcome a Sibling

To this day I remember the reaction of one-year-old Eric when I brought his baby brother, Todd, home from the hospital. When I tried to hug Eric, he stiffened and turned away. I was upset that he reacted that way, and I couldn't understand it. I didn't see the situation from his standpoint: not only had I left him, but I had returned with someone else—a younger, newer model!

It's hard for a child to go from being the center of your universe to having to share you with a new baby—who's getting most of your attention. Feelings of jealousy toward a new baby can be expressed in anger, aggression, withdrawal, or deliberate misbehavior. One mother told me that soon after his baby sister arrived, her four-year-old sat on the curb outside and refused to come in.

Remember, unless you had twins, your first child was an only child until you brought someone new home. Sharing someone you love isn't easy. Imagine if one day your husband announced that he loved you so much he was bringing home another wife (just a bit younger and cuter). I don't think you'd welcome her with open arms!

This is a time when your older child needs empathy and reassurance. Be sensitive to the signals that he might be feeling left out and in need of some special attention. For example, a three-year-old might express jealousy by interfering with your care of the baby or making demands on you just when you're starting a feeding or in the middle of changing a diaper. He may even express open hostility. Lois, a mother in one of my workshops, was very surprised when her three-year-old son, Anthony, cried, "I wish we could take that baby back! You don't even care about *me* anymore." But she wisely realized that Anthony needed immediate reassurance:

> **Mom:** Is that *really* the way you feel?
> **Anthony:** Yes! You're always taking care of *him*.
> **Mom:** Oh, honey, I'm *so* glad you told me. Let's just you and I do something fun together after lunch.
> **Anthony:** *(brightening)* Can we go to the playground?
> **Mom:** OK. Daddy can watch Ben.

When a young child feels upset about a new baby seeming to take over the household, he's letting you know that he needs some undivided attention. Take that extra minute to hear him.

Even older children can feel jealous and threatened when a new baby arrives. A six- or seven-year-old child may express those feelings by being sarcastic and critical of the baby, ignoring him, constantly complaining that you spend less time with her, or acting babyish and dependent. The best strategy is to acknowledge your child's feelings—"Yes, that baby sure does cry a lot"—while enlisting her involvement and praising her contribution. For example, you might say, "You're so good at making your brother laugh. I'll bet you can help me think of a way to entertain him."

A mother in my New York workshop lamented the unloving statements her first child, Jonathan, made about his baby sister: "I don't know why you think she's so cute. She looks like a bald old man." Naturally, Jonathan's mother was upset and said angrily, "You're never to talk about the baby like that. You're lucky you're not an only child like I was."

A more helpful response would be, "I guess sometimes the baby really annoys you. I understand." Empathy goes a long way toward making a child feel more secure and less angry. Many kids also feel guilty about their negative feelings for a new sibling. This

---

■ Parent's Story: The Interloper

"My son was very excited to have a baby sister. I took him to sibling classes at the hospital and told him that I would always love him, no matter what. He seemed satisfied. But as his sister got older, he became troubled. One day he asked me out of the blue, 'Why did you have to have her? Wasn't I good enough?'"

is an important time to help them distinguish between feelings and actions.

61. Engage Big Brother or Sister

Help your older child feel important by reinforcing his or her special status as the big brother or sister:

- Let your child help with small tasks where appropriate—feeding, changing, fetching, rocking, washing, holding.
- Ask your child to draw pictures for the baby, and put them above his or her crib.
- Make an effort to praise your eldest child's accomplishments, like toilet training. At the same time, expect and allow permission for babyish behavior on occasion.
- Show your child pictures of herself when she was a baby. Recall how excited you were with her arrival.
- In the eldest child's presence, tell your baby how great it is to have a big brother or sister who can make her laugh, get her things, or rock her gently.

Having a new baby in the house is usually exhausting and incredibly time-consuming. But for the sake of an older child, try your best to maintain a routine that is as close to the old one as possible. Be particularly sensitive to maintaining favorite rituals, like bedtime stories or games.

The sense of pride that comes with being a big brother or sister can last for a lifetime. As your younger child grows, you can

---

■ **Parent's Story: Jake's Fan Club**

Whenever Nick, my two-year-old, wants something fixed, I say to him, "Take it to Jake [my six-year-old]. He can do it for you." Jake will stop whatever he's doing and put the toy back together. He ends up feeling useful and loving to his younger brother, who of course thinks he's wonderful and looks up to him. I also say to Nick in front of Jake, "Nick, you're so lucky to have a big brother like Jake."

---

continue to encourage this special relationship. Look for opportunities to praise the older child when he's being thoughtful or responsible. Let him overhear you talking about him. For example, on the phone to your child's dad, you might say, "It's a good thing Jerry has a big brother like Pete. Pete was really watching out for him when we were at Aunt Ann's today." Or to a younger child, "Your big sister really loves to read to you. You're so lucky!"

62. Negotiate the Sibling Battle Zone

It's a fact. Siblings will fight, about everything and anything. It's not always such a bad thing and, believe it or not, even serves a worthwhile purpose. Sibling rivalry provides a way for kids to test their limits, assert themselves, and learn to negotiate for what they want and need—in the safety of their own home.

However, parents hate these squabbles, and it's very tempting to jump in and try to stop them. If this temptation is a big one for you—as it is for almost every parent—I urge you to do what you can to stay out of the middle. I know that's easier said than done. One mom I know puts on a Walkman to drown out the bickering when fights erupt, which makes fighting much less fun for the kids. Another parent, who is less tolerant of noise, has a harder time not intervening. I suggested he set a timer for four minutes when an argument began, and if the kids were still fighting when the timer went off, he should step in. To his surprise, he discovered the disputes rarely lasted the full four minutes, although the time seemed like hours to him.

Several parents have observed with dismay that when two or more siblings are bickering, the younger one rarely rises to the level of the older child; however, the older sibling often descends to the level of his little brother or sister. So, even if you have a six-year-old and a three-year-old, it often seems as though they're behaving like two three-year-olds! Don't anticipate that your older child will always act in a more mature way. It's probably more realistic to lower your expectations for your children to act maturely during these sibling squabbles.

You can't ignore fights if your children are about to hurt each other. At those times when they're becoming out of control, you have to remove them from each other. In addition to preventing the physical confrontation, separation also tends to remind them that they really want to be with each other. Hard feelings usually vanish. Within minutes of being separated, they're inching out of their rooms, eager to play together again.

■ Humor Break

When a mother told her three-year-old daughter, "I don't want to see you hitting your sister," her daughter replied, "Then close your eyes."

■ **Parent's Story: Car Fights**

"When my kids start fighting in the backseat of the car, I don't say a word. I just find a place to pull over, stop the car, get out, and walk a few feet away. Immediately, they stop fighting and start begging me to come back. It works every time."

When the fighting gets physical or emotionally hurtful, you will probably have to get involved. But avoid vague commands like, "Be nice," "Stop it," or "Can't you guys ever get along?" You're likely to hear, "I *am* being nice. He started it" or "You're always blaming *me*." Be specific about the behavior you don't like, and help your child come up with a solution, as Jan did with her five-year-old:

> **Jan:** David, hitting is not allowed in our house.
> **David:** But Lyle just wrecked my building. It took me *hours* to make it.
> **Jan:** I can see why you'd be furious. Did you tell him how angry you are?
> **David:** Yes, but he won't listen.
> **Jan:** Can you think of another way besides hitting to keep Lyle out of your stuff?
> **David:** Yeah. Keeping him out of my room.
> **Jan:** How will you do that?
> **David:** I'll put a big sign on my door: "Keep Out!"
> **Jan:** That's an idea. Why don't you try it? But no hitting.

Your goal here is to help them solve the problem, not to force your kids to love each other. You can't legislate love. You can only encourage cooperation.

■ **Simple Solution for Everyday Squabbles**

This suggestion comes from a mother of four.

First, ask your kids to make a list of all the things they fight about. The list might look like this:

- Who gets the window seat in the van
- Whose turn it is to use the computer
- Who gets to check the mailbox or the E-mail first
- Who chooses the video
- Who picks the restaurant when we eat out

Next, make a weekly chart, and divvy up the choices. Post the chart on the refrigerator. When in doubt, check the chart and resolve the squabble: "It says here that on Tuesday Matt chooses the video."

63. Don't Even *Try* to Be Fair

Most parents believe that being fair is an achievable goal. We think that if we treat all our children equally, they will eventually stop arguing about who got more, who gets to go first, or who's the favorite. The trouble is, they won't.

Fairness is not achievable—at least not in the way kids define it. Trying to treat children equally at every moment is like trying to extricate yourself from quicksand: the more you struggle, the deeper you sink. As one parent said when complaining about how her kids were habitually comparing everything, "It's as if they were born with a built-in fairness meter."

The truth is, your children don't really want to be treated the same at every moment, no matter how much they clamor for equality. The hidden message behind the fairness complaint is this:

"Am I special? Do you love me? Am I worthy of your attention?" For that reason, treating children identically often backfires. You end up depriving them of what they truly want, which is to be considered unique and valued for who they are.

Instead of trying to be perfectly fair, try these ways of showing each child she is special in your eyes.

Get Your Child to Focus on What *He* Wants, Not What His Sibling Got

Try to change the focus from comparison to individual need, as Celia did with six-year-old Matt:

Matt: Billy got more cereal than me.
Celia: You sound like you're really hungry.
Matt: I am!
Celia: OK. Show me how much more you want.

Of course, not all sibling inequities are as easy to solve. If there's only one piece of cake left with a rose decoration and three kids want it, there's no way to make everyone happy. Children will have to deal with the hard but unavoidable lesson that life isn't always fair. There's nothing wrong with saying, "Next time, it will be your turn." Be prepared for "next time," though, because children will call you on it.

To avoid a fight over such issues as who had what last and whose turn it is next, let your kids work out a schedule for whose turn it is to play with a favorite toy, use the computer, or choose the TV channel. Then post the rotation on the refrigerator.

A mother of two told me how she dealt with one situation. When Grandma came for a week's visit, she would take each child separately for a day trip, beginning with the oldest. The younger one complained that it was not fair she always had to go last. The mother gave her a hug and said, "Sometimes you wish you were the oldest so she'd take you first." However, once Grammy became aware of her youngest granddaughter's complaint, she varied the outings between the two of them.

Respond to Unique Needs with Unique Treatment

Few things push a parent's guilt buttons more than the accusation "You love him more!" Complaints of favoritism can put you on the defensive, but remember: your children do not need to be treated the same. Allow yourself to respond to them according to their different ages, personalities, abilities, and moods. The trick is to explain this in a way your children can understand.

When her new baby monopolized Eileen's time, four-year-old Linda said accusingly, "You're always picking that baby up. You never pick me up. You love her more than me."

■ Parent's Story: Playing Favorites

Monica, a mother in one of my parent workshops, was embarrassed to admit that she often felt more loving toward her two-year-old son than his four-year-old sister. "Eli is such an agreeable child," she said. "He's so much easier to deal with than his sister, who can be so whiny. I'm always secretly wishing that Katie were more like Eli."

I told Monica to accept her feelings as natural. Sometimes you just can't help but relate better to one child than another because his temperament more closely resembles yours. It's also hard *not* to favor the child who is easier to handle. However, I urged her to try to separate what she felt from how she treated her children: "Don't overlook the child you have less of an affinity for. Make sure that you notice and express appreciation for her unique qualities and talents."

Eileen kept her explanation simple: "I love you both very much. The baby needs me to hold her and feed her and change her. You need me to read you stories and tuck you in at night. But I do want to spend more time with you. As soon as I put the baby down for a nap, let's play a game together."

It's unrealistic to expect that you can completely end children's accusations that you're not being fair. But by responding to each child's unique qualities, you can send the message that it is possible to be fair without trying to make everything even.

■ Parent's Story: All's Fair in Love and War

A mother told me this story about her two sons.

"Greg came running to me crying, 'Jonathan threw a rock at me!' I was furious, and I demanded, 'Jonathan, how *could* you?' Jonathan replied, 'Well, he threw one at me first!' When I turned to Greg for an explanation, he cried, 'Yeah, but *mine* missed!'"

---

64. Avoid Comparing Your Kids

When they were young, my sons, Eric and Todd, were different in every way. Eric tended to be more careful. He was cautious about new situations. Todd, on the other hand, was impulsive and eager to jump into new situations with both feet—often without worrying about consequences. It baffled me that two children born of the same parents and being raised under the same roof could be so very different. How easily I had forgotten how different my own brother and I were!

Parents must be constantly aware that their children will be more different than similar. Like me, parents are sometimes unprepared for that fact.

Most parents today are aware that comparing children increases sibling rivalry. But sometimes, especially when we're frustrated with our more challenging child, we let it slip, with comments such as, "Why can't you be more like your sister? She doesn't argue with every single thing I say" or "Jimmy gets good grades at school because he studies so hard. Maybe you should try that, too."

Also be careful to avoid slipping into comparisons when you're talking about your children to a third party. Kids have remarkable radar when they're being discussed. I remember when I was on the phone talking to a friend about how much harder it was for Eric to try new things than for Todd. I wasn't speaking loudly, and Eric was at least three rooms away, but he appeared immediately at my side and resentfully denied it.

Even a compliment can backfire when phrased as a comparison, such as, "Your sister is the brain in the family, and you're the comedian." Statements like this spark feelings of rivalry and resentment among children, as well as giving them the impression that you prefer one to the other. As soon as I hear a parent say, "My younger one is such an angel—happy, sociable, easygoing," I get concerned that what I'll hear next is "But my older one—he's impossible. He drives me nuts." Kids are reflections of the mirrors we hold up to them, and these kinds of labels reinforce the very behavior we want to discourage. It also restricts them to act according to these labels—especially the negative ones. To this day Mary, who was quite shy as a child, remembers being called a wallflower by her father. She's thirty-eight now and that label often comes to mind when she's in certain social situations.

Keep in mind that feelings of favoritism can ebb and flow as your children grow and change. The adorable toddler becomes the demanding four-year-old; the hard-to-please preschooler blossoms into the confident and adaptable first-grader. The child who is difficult one year may be a real pleasure the next.

Part of the excitement of having more than one child is discovering who each new individual will be and seeing how the next child differs from the last. Real family life is a crazy quilt of multiple faces, styles, quirks, personalities, preferences, problems, and talents. Even though we sometimes wish it could be simpler—and bite our tongues so as not to say, "Why can't you be more like your brother?"—most parents agree that they wouldn't really want their children to be carbon copies of one another. In fact, we can find delight and satisfaction in the adventure of discovering their differences.

65. Raise a Happy Only Child

If you're the parent of one child, you've probably heard the negative rap about only children. A lot of people in our society assume that an only child will be lonely because he doesn't have siblings, selfish because he doesn't have to share his things with brothers and sisters, and spoiled because he is lavished with undivided parental attention. There is a sense, too, that the best thing parents can do for an only is to present him with a brother or sister—that his experience of life will always be incomplete without a sibling. I've even heard people say that they didn't feel as if they were a complete family until they had more than one child. (Remember, first children are onlies for a while, too.)

These fears only lead to parental guilt and unhealthy efforts to overcompensate for an only's supposed disadvantages by giving her too much attention or too many material things. In fact, the development of positive self-esteem and successful social skills does not depend on a child having siblings. Having brothers and sisters may be a wonderful thing, but being an only child also has a lot of advantages.

There are, however, unique issues that parents of only children must address, just as there are unique issues for parents of siblings. The following tips can help you avoid some of the potential pitfalls.

Don't Be Hypervigilant

An only child sometimes has the impression that all of the rays of the sun are shining on her. Such an intense spotlight is daunting for a child because children need the space to grow and develop their own sense of self, apart from their parents.

Sometimes parents of only children are afflicted with the "only chance" syndrome. They become excessively cautious and overly protective, afraid to allow their kids to take risks or experience any consequences. Here are some tips for avoiding that pitfall:

- Allow your child to experiment and explore—away from you.
- Remember that all parents (even those with several children) feel nervous the first time a child rides a bus by herself or walks to the corner store alone.
- Once you're sure your child has practiced your safety rules, try not to let your fears show. Instead, try to keep your anxiety under wraps. You want your child to feel competent—which she can't do if you're hovering.

Encourage Diverse Relationships

It is not necessarily true that an only child is going to feel lonely. While siblings do supply immediate companionship in the household, most of us realize that loneliness can be experienced in crowds, too. It is the quality of relationships, not their quantity, that makes the greatest impact. However, parents of one child may need to make an extra effort to foster relationships outside the home:

- Maintain as much contact as you can with members of your extended family. Let your child know that his grandparents, aunts, uncles, and cousins are part of his family, even when they don't live nearby. One mother I know, who encouraged many regular visits with relatives, was thrilled when her eight-year-old son became pen pals with his cousin from across the country. They developed a brotherly relationship that grew over the years, without the rivalry inherent in most sibling relationships.

- Involve your child in play groups and other activities at an early age. Learning to socialize with peers is a basic lesson for children. When your child has many opportunities to be with other children, she can practice social skills. It's also one of the best ways to teach her that her needs don't always come first.

- If you begin to feel guilty because you suspect your child feels lonely without siblings, remember that almost every child with siblings sometimes wishes she were an only.

- Make your home a comfortable, warm, welcoming place for your child's friends and playmates.

Finally, as the parent of an only child, give yourself permission to enjoy the positives, rather than focusing on the pitfalls.

Numerous studies have shown that only children can be just as well balanced, happy, creative, caring, and bright as children with siblings—sometimes even more so.

66. Put the Tattletale Out of Business

I remember well how I used to love informing my mother of the bad things my brother was doing. It made me feel so virtuous. Unfortunately, I didn't succeed at getting Tommy in trouble, because my mother hated tattling. Whenever I tried, she would say, "The one who tattles will get in trouble." I wasn't happy with her response, but it ended my tattling.

Tattling is a common tactic when siblings jockey for position over who will get the "favored child" status. Usually, the goal of the tattletale is to get a brother or sister in trouble, thus making the tattler appear more angelic. Some parents instinctively understand, as my mother did, that tattlers are rarely innocent parties. However, since parents are often busy or distracted, they may respond automatically. Jerry cries, "Dad! I saw Rick playing with your new tools," and Dad has a knee-jerk reaction: "Rick, you get in here this instant! I told you not to touch those tools. There will be no TV for you tonight!" (You can be sure that Jerry has a smug smile on his face.)

Joyce, the mother of a boy and a girl, ages eight and five, described to me how she finally cured her daughter of incessant tattling. "She was always shouting, 'I'm *telling!*' and I'd just dread it because it meant I had to stop what I was doing and deal with it. One day I was on the phone, and Molly ran in shrieking, 'Mom! Mom! Kevin is eating all the chocolate-chip cookies!'

Instead of immediately hanging up as I had in the past, I turned to her and said, 'Please don't interrupt me while I'm on the phone.' She looked surprised, but she quieted down. After I hung up, I said, 'If your brother is in danger of hurting himself or you, you can tell me about it. Otherwise I don't want to hear about it.' She was stunned. But every time she tattled on Kevin, I kept reinforcing it by saying, 'Is he in danger? Are you in danger?' And finally she stopped."

This mother had the right idea. Sometimes children will get on a roll—especially if Mom or Dad cooperates—and automatically scream out any infraction their sibling commits. It can be quite tedious. I loved the solution a skillful elementary school teacher used for the constant tattling in her third-grade class. She made a rule that any complaint about another child must be put in writing. Needless to say, most of the kids didn't want to go to the time and trouble of writing down their complaints. It took all the satisfaction out of telling.

When a child runs to you crying about some terrible injustice inflicted by a sibling, don't get trapped into taking sides. And when you *do*, don't let the tattler get the satisfaction of seeing you run in to attack the so-called guilty one.

We don't have to (nor can we) always make our children's upset feelings disappear. Sometimes it's enough to let kids know they're being taken seriously. That's the approach Marcie used with her daughter Annie:

> **Annie:** She called me a bad name, and I wasn't doing anything!
>
> **Marcie:** I bet you'd like me to go yell at her.
>
> **Annie:** Yeah!
>
> **Marcie:** And you'd like me to punish her severely.
>
> **Annie:** Yeah!
>
> **Marcie:** I know. She really makes you mad. Sometimes it's not easy having a younger sister.

I encourage parents to stay out of the middle of sibling spats, whenever possible. When one child yells, "Mommeee, he called me a name!" and the other, "She started it!" chances are they're bored and want your attention. When you do step in, exonerating one and chastising the other, be prepared for another fight to erupt soon afterward.

Remember, kids aren't as busy as you are. They have plenty of time to find creative ways of getting you to take sides. Be aware that their goal in tattling is to get you to take their side or get their sibling in trouble—always a no-win situation for all of you.

67. Resist the Urge to Futurize

Parents often fear their children will never be friends. Observing the daily battles that rage between her two sons, one mother told me, "My kids hate each other. I don't think they'll ever get along." She admitted that her thoughts were full of grim future scenarios, where her sons refused to attend family gatherings together and wouldn't have anything to do with each other.

"I wanted more than one child so my children could be companions for life," she said sadly. "I was so wrong." She sounded completely dejected. When I pressed for more details, I was surprised to learn her sons were only six and eight. I told her, "It's always a mistake to use the F-word: *futurize*. Children change constantly and are different from one year to the next—and even from one week to the next. That applies to their relationships as siblings, too."

Undoubtedly, this mother's fears were premature, but I could understand her feelings. When my sons were young, I remember vividly how I feared that they would never love each other. I imagined them in the future, as adults, refusing to speak, except to insult one another. These imaginings made me feel like quite a failure as a parent. I thought if I were a better mother, my sons would fight less and love one another more.

Only later did I learn that their rivalry was normal and, ultimately, harmless. Today, Eric and Todd are extremely close. They talk on the phone nearly every day and have a remarkable bond. They like and respect each other. I never would have imagined twenty years ago that they'd be such great friends now. Watching my sons together, I realize that my fears of old were unfounded. I also failed to see that the bonds of loyalty between children don't always look the way we think they should. If I had it to do all over again, I would spend far less time agitating about tomorrow and more time enjoying today.

In my third book, *Loving Each One Best*, I quoted a parent of grown children who said it best: "They used to kill each other; now they'd kill *for* each other."

■ Parent's Story: A Moment of Truth

Sometimes you see a different side of sibling animosity when you catch a glimpse of your kids while they don't know you're watching. A mother told me this story about her two children.

"My eight-year-old son complained bitterly about having to put up with his 'bratty' five-year-old sister. I was feeling very discouraged. However, the same day he told me how much he hated his sister, I looked out the window and saw him patiently teaching her how to throw and catch a ball."

PART 8

■

Teach Social Skills

68. Curb Your Rude Dude

Under the tutelage of his six-year-old brother, two-and-a-half-year-old Jason has added a new word to his vocabulary: *butthead*. Every time he says it, Jason's brother and his friends collapse into spasms of laughter. Then one day, as Jason and his mother were leaving a shoe store, the salesclerk, a kindly older woman who had fitted Jason with new boots, gave him a balloon as she said good-bye. "Good-bye, butthead," he called out with gusto. The woman gasped, the smile frozen on her face.

This is a situation that could make even the most laid-back parent cringe. Although Jason's response is unacceptable and needs to be addressed, it's understandable in light of his brother's encouragement and enthusiastic coaching.

Very young children rarely know when they're being rude. Sometimes toddlers and young children say things that are rude but funny. Or rude but true. Or just plain rude. Whether it's the precocious use of a four-letter word or an innocent truth, such as "Grandma has a really big nose," kids seem to know just what to say to curl your hair. Such statements don't necessarily mean that your child is rude—just young.

However, as children approach school age, they become cognizant of how their words affect other people. A five-year-old who makes an insulting remark is old enough to be reprimanded and to offer an apology.

Even though a young child may not understand why certain words hurt, she will begin to learn empathy by seeing your negative reaction to those words, by hearing you say, "I'm sorry," on her behalf, and by seeing you model kindness. With older children, you can even turn such awkward moments into opportunities to teach compassion and diplomacy.

Although people may disagree on exactly what constitutes rudeness, it is very easy to define politeness. Politeness is simply a basic respect for the feelings of others.

Teach Toddlers Basic Courtesy

When children start talking, it's inevitable that they will quickly pick up unsavory language from older siblings, friends, television, and people on the street. One good way to head off embarrassing outbursts is to monitor your own language. For example, if your child hears you utter a certain expletive when another driver cuts you off on the highway, I can guarantee that he'll use the same word at full volume the next time he's at a family gathering. There-

---

■ **Parent's Story: Garbage Mouth**

To discourage her three-year-old daughter from using slang, Carol decided that slang goes in the garbage. Here's a typical scenario:

Mom: Samantha, would you like some juice?
Samantha: Yeah.
Mom: Uh-oh—what's *yeah*?
Samantha: Slang!
Mom: And what do we do with slang?
Samantha: We throw it in the garbage!

They then pretend to grab the word out of the air and to toss it into the garbage.

---

fore, if *butthead* is off-limits for Jason, it should be off-limits for everyone in the family.

When your young child does come out with an embarrassing statement, you should calmly apologize for him. Jason's mother might have said to the saleswoman, "I'm sorry about what Jason said. That was very rude of him."

It's never too early to teach your kids to say "excuse me," "please," "thank you," "may I," "good morning," and other courtesies. When Ricardo, two and a half, said to his mother, "Gimme some yogurt," Mom replied, "That's not how we talk. When you want some yogurt, what you say is 'Mommy, may I please have some yogurt?'"

Practice Telephone Skills with Your Child

Teach your children how you want them to answer the phone and how to take a message politely. You can make this fun if you role-play with them. Instead of "Huh?" or "What?," let them practice saying, "May I help you?" and "Can I take a message?" Encourage your children to repeat the caller's name and, once they are able, to clearly write down the person's name and telephone number. Whenever I telephone a parent and her child answers politely, I make it a point to compliment the parent afterward.

Teach Respect at Home

You're not doing your child any favors by allowing her to address you in a disrespectful manner. If your child has gotten into the habit of being rude to you, you may want to dock her allowance for each infraction or withdraw certain privileges. Whatever route you try, you must make it clear that you will not be treated rudely. You may want to say something along the lines of "You can be angry, and you can even hate me, and you can hate the rules around here. But I will not be spoken to that way."

Teaching children politeness is one of the ongoing (and least glamorous) jobs of being a parent. It takes practice and repetition. And it's so much harder today, when other adults are so rude and are constantly models of discourtesy—not answering when you say hello or cursing on the street in front of kids. What's more, children are bombarded by a media blitz of vulgarity, meanness, intolerance, and "trash talk." One mother told me of taking her five-year-old daughter to a luncheonette. Her daughter noticed a sign that read "No Smoking" and said to the waitress, "It should say, 'No Smoking, *Please.*'" The waitress snapped at her, "What business is it of yours?!"

As difficult as it is to combat rudeness, the rewards are worth the effort. A child who knows how to behave in public or how to disagree politely with an adult is more confident in new situations—and a lot more pleasant to be around. What a gift we give our children by teaching them to treat other people with consideration, and considerate children are happier children.

69. Teach Street Smarts

The world has become a dangerous place for a child, and all parents worry about safety. We want to help our children recognize and avoid danger without making them fearful, withdrawn, or in a constant state of anxiety.

A healthy suspicion of strangers is an important element of street smarts. Introduce guidelines for dealing with strangers the same way you would teach your kids to look both ways before crossing the street—clearly and straightforwardly. Make sure they understand that the majority of people aren't dangerous. Your goal is to educate, not to scare them.

The Basic Rules

Be sure to explain just what a "stranger" is. Don't assume your child knows. Then go over the basics:

- Unless you are with a parent, don't answer questions from a person you don't know.
- Don't agree to help a stranger, even if he seems upset or in trouble. Get a trusted grown-up to call for help instead.
- Don't answer the door unless you recognize the person's voice or can see who it is through the peephole.
- If a stranger offers you candy, gifts, or a ride, or asks you to help him find his lost puppy, say no and run away. If a stranger, relative, baby-sitter, or family friend tries to touch you or makes you feel funny, tell a parent or teacher right away.
- When you're alone in the house, if someone unfamiliar calls and asks, "Is your mother home?" reply, "She can't come to the phone. May I take a message?"

Allow plenty of time to talk to your child about safety rules. Don't wait until he's about to go out the door by himself. A child of five or six is able to understand these guidelines.

Practice Scenarios

Use what-ifs to get information across. Turning the message into a game keeps kids' interest and also helps them to develop good judgment and a wide range of effective responses. Besides learning what *not* to do, children learn what they *can* do. Ask them the three basic problem-solving questions:

"What would happen if . . . ?"
"What can you do if . . . ?"
"What else can you do?"

Example 1: "Pretend you've just walked into the boy's bathroom at school. A man is in there and starts asking you questions. What would you do?"

Example 2: "We're at the supermarket, and Mommy is in the next aisle. A woman walks up to you and says, 'We're giving free candy to all the children in the store. Come with me, and I'll give you some.' What would you do?"

Use role-playing to emphasize points. Pretend to be the stranger while your child practices various responses. Here are some of the options you might discuss together:

• Saying, "No, thank you," or "Stop that," or just, "No!"
• Saying, "I don't know you," and walking away
• Running away
• Telling a trusted grown-up
• Yelling for help
• Shouting, "You're not my mother/father!"

Kids Should Trust Their Instincts

It's very important for parents to understand that children can, by nature, sense danger. If we talk them out of their instinctive feelings, they will no longer trust those feelings. For example, a child brought up to be polite, obey grown-ups, and say yes when she means no will have a hard time turning down a stranger who says, "Little girl, will you help me find my kitty?"

▨ Parent's Story: Mixed Messages

The first time her son John went to the store alone, Cheryl learned that her safety messages weren't always clear. Before John left the house, Cheryl launched into what she calls her Stranger Talk: "Be very careful. Don't talk to anyone you don't know. If they offer you candy, don't take it. If someone asks you a question, don't answer. And if a stranger offers you a ride in a car, don't get in." When she was done, she asked John if he had any questions.

"Mommy," he said, eyes sparkling, "somebody is going to give me candy?"

Encourage your child to trust her instincts. Parents can use the following statements to reinforce that lesson:

> "If you have a funny feeling about someone, or if anything another person does makes you feel uncomfortable, trust your feelings. It's OK to say no and run away, even if it means being rude."
> "If somebody wants to kiss or touch you, and you don't want them to, you don't have to let them, even if it's someone you know."

Listen carefully to your child. She may try to talk to you but not have the right words to explain what's happened. A child might say, "That person was bothering me," but not know how to explain the reason for her discomfort. Make sure she feels safe telling you if she's uncomfortable, nervous, or scared. Reassure her that you won't be angry or upset. You can best protect her if she knows that she can talk to you about anything without fear of being criticized.

70. Make Manners Matter

Believe it or not, kids want to know how to behave well. In any social situation involving adults, they are uncomfortable when left to their own devices, without guidelines. In teaching them manners, we empower children by showing them how to get along in the world.

Here's what you can expect from your children in terms of age-appropriate manners.

Toddlers and Two-Year-Olds

The idea of manners doesn't really exist for two-year-olds. If they're tired or unhappy, they're going to cry or whine. If they're bored, they will squirm. If they're asked to do something they don't feel like doing, they'll refuse. However, even parents who know that their child tends to be shy around strangers may become anxious that he won't shine brightly in the eyes of guests and relatives. We have friends whose son won't talk or make eye contact until he's been around us for at least an hour. His parents are very cool about it. They don't try to force him, and there's no tension.

When young children get fussy, remove them from the spotlight. Don't try to force them to perform or expect them to be comfortable with strangers.

Three- to Five-Year-Olds

Kids under the age of six are fundamentally egocentric. Thinking about other people's needs or feelings doesn't come naturally to them. Therefore, when you tell them to act nicely or be polite, they need to know exactly what you mean. Try to be as specific as possible—even giving your child the exact words to say in different situations. Remember, one of the most fun and effective ways to prepare kids for new situations is to role-play with them.

Look for opportunities to let your child practice being polite to others, such as holding the door for a shopper or saying please and thank you. One mother told the story of riding the bus with her son. Noticing an elderly woman standing, she pulled her son onto her lap so the woman could sit down. He protested loudly at being denied his own seat. She held him tight and acknowledged his feelings but didn't give him a choice. He didn't have to like it, but he was learning a lesson in courtesy just the same.

Six- to Ten-Year-Olds

By the time a child is six, she can be expected to adhere to basic rules of consideration. When elementary school–aged children deliberately behave rudely—adopting a scornful expression; saying, "That's stupid!"; or adding a sarcastic tone to every question and comment—it's often because they like the feeling of challenging adult authority. In large family gatherings, they may also behave this way to show off in front of other kids. None of these explanations, however, makes rude behavior OK. Make clear to your kids that it won't be tolerated.

Eight-year-old Samantha wasn't looking forward to the impending visit of her grandparents. "Grandpa is so boring. All he does is tell the same old dumb stories," she complained. Samantha's mother hated to hear her daughter speak disrespectfully about her grandfather, even though it was true that he did tend to tell the same anecdotes over and over again. She resolved matters by talking to Samantha the day before he arrived:

> **Mom:** Grandpa is probably going to tell his fish story again—about how he caught the big one.

Samantha: Oh, no. I'm sick of hearing that story!

Mom: Yes, we've all heard it a million times. But, you know, it makes him so happy to tell it. Why don't we let Grandpa have his moment in the sun? I know I can count on you to do that for Grandpa.

Instead of saying, "Don't you speak about your grandfather that way," this mom empathized with her daughter's valid observation, while asking her to do something she didn't want to do for the sole reason that it would make someone else happy. Preparing Samantha in advance enabled her to be more considerate toward her grandfather.

Like most things, good manners take practice, and it's never too early to start. In my workshops, some parents teach kids as young as two or three to say, "Excuse me," and to ask politely for what they want. These efforts are never wasted. If you can pass along the crucial message of caring and consideration, you'll have taught your child real manners—not the kind that come from a book, but the kind that come from the heart.

71. Minimize Holiday Stresses

For most adults, Thanksgiving, Christmas, Passover, Kwanzaa, and Ramadan are the ultimate family gatherings—times when we dream about loved ones coming together in joyous celebration, to store up wonderful memories for the future. The trouble is, holidays—compounded by a house full of company, disrupted routines, and too much excitement—often bring out the worst in our children. Though we know how sweet, funny, and lovable our kids can be, we worry that relatives and guests may only see their overexcited, cranky, thoughtless side.

Here are some suggestions for minimizing those holiday stresses.

Maintain Familiar Routines

Young children require a sense of order and predictability, and that's hard to achieve when you have guests, and even more so when you're visiting friends and family. Figure out in advance what adjustments you need to make to be sure that your child's daily schedule stays the same—or as close to it as possible. For example, if your two-year-old normally takes a nap at one in the afternoon, try to arrange for that to happen, even if it means you have to lie down with him. Take along familiar foods, and be sure he has his comfort toys on hand.

Don't Force Them to Shine

If your little one bursts into tears at the sight of Grandpa, refuses to give Grandma a kiss, or won't sing her favorite song out loud to the assembled throng, don't push her. Don't make excuses. And don't feel disappointed. She's just being a two-year-old. I remember being so proud of Eric when he memorized a nursery rhyme and loved saying it—until I tried to get him to repeat it for my mother. No way!

Stay Close By

Your young child may be particularly clingy when you're in a strange house or when there are visitors in your home. In a room full of unfamiliar people, she needs you close by. Reassure her that you're watching out for her. It will help her feel safer in the presence of others.

Tell Children in Advance Exactly What to Expect

If you're flying to a faraway destination, talk about what happens in an airport, how long the trip will take, what it's like to be on a plane, and how you expect your kids to act while traveling by air. If you'll be staying at a relative's house, describe the scene and establish ground rules: "You'll be sleeping in Cousin Carol's room. There will be a lot of people there you've never met." Show pictures of relatives in advance and talk about them. "This is Uncle George. He's a doctor just like Doctor Stone. Grandma doesn't hear very well, so when you talk to her, remember that you have to stand close to her ear."

Give Your Child the Right Words to Say

Practicing beforehand can help young children say or do the right thing. For instance, you can tell your son in advance, "Aunt Margaret goes to so much trouble every year making a big holiday dinner, and there will be lots of different kinds of food at her house. Some of them will seem strange to you. She may offer you something you don't like. If you say, 'That's yucky,' or, 'These beans taste slimy,' that will hurt her feelings and make her very upset. All you have to do instead is say, 'No, thank you, Aunt Margaret.'"

Have a Backup Plan

No matter how well you orchestrate your visits to and from relatives, you must prepare for the unexpected when you have young children. If you attend a church, mosque, or synagogue during religious holidays, check in advance to see if there are separate, supervised areas where kids can go if they get fidgety. Or if you know your five-year-old will turn up his nose at the gourmet goodies at your sister's Christmas dinner, feed him in advance.

Many of us get caught up envisioning the perfect holiday scene with the entire family worshiping together or sitting as a happy group at the table. These idealistic images are usually based on a fantasy—perhaps even one we had before our children came into the world!

If you're mired in a rut of family obligations and traditions that bring more stress than pleasure, you'll find many helpful suggestions in Elaine St. James's book, *Simplify Your Christmas* (Andrews McMeel, 1998). The subtitle, *100 Ways to Reduce the Stress and Recapture the Joy of the Holidays*, really fulfills its promise. By meeting together as a family and rethinking the traditions that are truly significant, and giving up those that create more anxiety than pleasure, you'll create new, more meaningful rituals to pass on to your children.

72. Stifle Your Embarrassment

Diplomacy is an acquired skill, but most parents would prefer their kids learned it sooner rather than later. The mother of a four-year-old once confided to me, "I don't want him to be *totally* honest. I want him to be *selectively* honest." I knew exactly what she meant. We all know that kids say the darnedest things, but we often find that the remarks sound much cuter when they're coming from the mouth of someone else's child. Often it's the audience more than the performance that makes us uncomfortable.

I had to laugh at the child who told her mother's elderly friend that she smelled good. The lady replied, "Thank you. That's my new toilet water." Horrified, the little girl said, "You've gotta be kidding. You got water from the toilet?!"

Miranda, a mom in one of my workshops, told us that visiting her in-laws always made her anxious. She just couldn't shake the feeling that she was on display as a mother, constantly being judged by the behavior of her two-year-old daughter, Keri. Miranda's fears caused her endless tension since Keri was a typical toddler—unpredictable and uninhibited.

During one visit, Keri was happily perched on her grandma's lap when she suddenly reached up and patted her cheek. "What's that all over your face?" she demanded loudly. Miranda turned bright red when she realized what Keri was asking, and she was about to jump in and say something to her daughter. But her mother-in-law beat her to it: "Why, honey," the older woman said, laughing, "those are called wrinkles."

Much of the time, young children don't intend to be rude when they ask embarrassing questions. Often they're just gathering information: *Why does that boy have only one leg? Why is that lady's nose crooked? Where is that man's hair? Why is he wearing a patch over his eye? Does the lady with a big belly have a baby in her tummy?* When young children ask these kinds of questions, they really want to know the answers.

For instance, you're in the park with your four-year-old son when he notices that the man at the hot-dog stand has only a stump for a left hand. Your son remarks loudly, "Oh, ick! Why doesn't he have regular fingers?" Your natural temptation might be to drag your child away or scold him for being rude. But you would miss a good teaching opportunity. In this case, politely say to the vendor, "My son doesn't mean to be rude. He's just trying to understand what happened to your hand."

If the man seems willing, let him explain for himself. The answer can give your child valuable information about differences among people—for example, "I was in an accident, and I lost my hand," or, "I was born without any fingers." Later, you can take your child aside and say, "I know you have questions when you see something you don't understand. But sometimes people don't like to be asked about why they're different. The next time you have a question, wait until we're alone and we can discuss it."

One picture book I recommend to parents of young children (three to six years) explains differences in a helpful, matter-of-fact way. It's called *Why Does That Man Have Such a Big Nose?* (Parenting Press, 1986), by Mary Beth Quinsey.

Finally, try to stifle your embarrassment when your young child blurts out an impolite statement or shamelessly asks a bold question of a stranger. Think of it as a teachable moment—a chance for your child to learn something important about the world and the diverse human beings who inhabit it.

73. Talk Back to Peer Pressure

Unless you move your family to Antarctica, you can't totally isolate kids from popular culture and negative peer influences, but you have more power to influence your children than you may realize. Our kids—especially as they reach puberty—may act as if they discount whatever we say, but they observe our values and they watch us carefully. They're more likely to be influenced if we speak to them without preaching.

To be effective in this sticky area, however, parents must never underestimate the power of the peer group. In one of his speeches, Dr. Mel Levine, a pioneer in the field of learning differences (www.allkindsofminds.com), expressed this eloquently: "Social success with peers is of paramount importance to most schoolchildren. The avoidance of humiliation at all costs is a relentless campaign . . . By middle school, social pressure reaches its greatest intensity, and children become vulnerable, self-conscious, aware of stereotyped gender roles, and eager not to deviate from behavioral norms."

Here are some guidelines for helping your child deal with the tricky aspects of peer pressure.

Offer Guidance

Fortunately, our children are likely to encounter positive peer pressure from the kids whose values we admire. However, when we think of peer pressure, we more often think of the negative kind. We worry that negative peer pressure will undo all of our efforts to teach positive values. But it's normal for children as they get older to test our values and try on behaviors and attitudes that we disapprove of. At the same time, children will still look to us for moral guidance, no matter how often they accuse us of being hopelessly "uncool." However, if you want to get your point across, avoid any statement that starts with "When I was your age . . ."

Example: You overhear your eleven-year-old daughter and her girlfriend making disparaging remarks about a new classmate. You're distressed to hear your normally thoughtful daughter speaking this way. Yet it would be a mistake to attack her in front of her friend by saying, "What's gotten into you? You used to be such a thoughtful person—not someone who'd make fun of other kids." Instead, calmly mention the incident when the two of you are alone. You might say, "I was surprised to overhear the way you were talking about the new girl in your class. You're usually so compassionate. It must be hard for her to come to a different school where she doesn't know anybody."

Keep in mind that your daughter may be afraid of being rejected by the "in" group if she doesn't join in the teasing. And preteens will go to great lengths to avoid being singled out or teased. Parents need to be sensitive to the enormous pressure on middle school–aged kids to fit in. One mom I know encourages her child not to bully a more vulnerable child by saying, "It takes a lot of guts not to go along with your friends when you realize they're being cruel."

Teach Your Children to Stand Up for Themselves

When your child faces a problem with a friend or classmate, the best thing you can do is help him figure out how to handle the problem on his own. Don't try to fight his battles for him, you'll risk making him feel powerless with his peers.

Example: Your nine-year-old complains that a classmate picks on him every day. Instead of expressing outrage, help him try to work out a solution. That's not easy—hearing that your child is being teased is excruciatingly painful since you have little control over the way other kids treat him. But children have to struggle and learn how to deal with put-downs. What you *can* do is provide a safe sounding board.

You might also brainstorm possible comebacks. Suggest he try making a joke, ignoring the classmate, or standing up to him. Role-playing is a very effective strategy to help your child figure out a response that may work for him. In her book, *Too Smart for Trouble* (Human Resource Development Press, 1990), Sharon Scott suggests many different and specific ways to deal with peers, recognizing that each child has to discover his or her own comfort level.

Praise Your Child for Doing the Right Thing

Recognize that it's very difficult for a child to take an independent position in the midst of a group. The child who learns to limit the influence of peers is the true leader with a steady moral compass.

Example: Your daughter sticks up for an overweight kid who is being picked on. Don't take her response for granted or say, "Well, I expect you to do the right thing." Instead, express your admiration. Tell her, "I'm proud of you for sticking up for Rachel. That showed courage."

Give Your Child a Way to Save Face

If your child is away from home and finds himself in a situation that is scary or uncomfortable, he may be reluctant to call you, fearing his friends will think he's not cool. You can help him save face by establishing a secret phone code that means "Come and pick me up right away."

Example: Fifteen-year-old Steve was at a party where there was a lot of drinking. Under the guise of calling another friend, he dialed his home number and said to his mom, "What time is soccer practice tomorrow?" It was their prearranged code that meant she should come and get him.

Be a Role Model

Finally, since kids take their cues from what we do, not just what we say, model the behaviors you're encouraging in your child. Let

him hear you speaking with respect and empathy toward others—
especially people who are different from you. Intolerance and
prejudice are very catching.

74. Beat the "Everybody Else" Syndrome

All kids—whether or not they have siblings as "rivals"—compare
themselves with friends, television characters, and other children
they observe on the street and playground. They notice what
other kids are wearing, what they're watching, and what they're
allowed to do and not to do. How do you handle complaints of
unfairness in a loving but firm way? The secret is to acknowledge
your child's complaints while still standing your ground.

When you do set these kinds of limits, be very clear. You
don't need to overexplain or justify every rule. And be prepared
for your kids to be upset or resentful. You're not their friend or
their grandparent!

As we've discussed throughout this book, your job is to be
unpopular with your children. I like what Dan Kindlon says in
his important new book, *Too Much of a Good Thing: Raising Children of Character in an Indulgent Age* (Hyperion, 2001): "We hate
when they're upset, and we don't want to deny ourselves the
pleasure of seeing them happy. As a result, we end up making
them feel that they're at the center of all universes, not just our
family."

Remember, giving your kids the ability to cope with disappointment and to tolerate frustration is doing them an important
favor. Just don't expect their gratitude until they're grown!

■ What to Say to "Everybody Else" Statements

YOUR CHILD SAYS . . .	DO NOT REPLY . . .	DO RESPOND . . .
"Everybody else's mom lets them watch TV after school."	"I'm not everyone else's mom. As long as you live here, you'll obey my rules."	"Well, in our house, the TV stays off until after homework is done."
"I need those sneakers. I have to have them. All my friends are wearing them."	"That's ridiculous. You don't have to have everything your friends have."	"I can see why you'd want those sneakers. Don't you wish they weren't so expensive? Let's keep our eyes open for a sale."
"Joey's mom lets him stay up until 9:30. Why can't I?"	"You're not Joey. He probably doesn't wake up grumpy like you do."	"On school nights you need your sleep. You can stay up later on the weekend."
"Julie's mom is nicer than you. She lets her have cookies any time."	"Why don't you go live at Julie's house, if you feel that way?"	"You'd like that, too, but in our house cookies are for after dinner."
"I'm the only one who isn't allowed to see that movie."	"Well, I don't know what those other parents are thinking. It's way too violent."	"I know you're disappointed. Is there something else we can do?"

75. Help Cultivate Positive Friendships

Peer relationships are vital to children's development. It's the arena in which they learn to make decisions, to lead or follow, to become considerate and loyal, and to recover from mistakes. As parents we can have some influence over our children's choice of friends. Here's how you can be helpful while still encouraging your child's independence.

De-Emphasize Popularity

Many parents unwittingly pressure their kids to make friends. They fret if their children aren't invited to every birthday party. They are devastated whenever their kids are rejected by the "in" crowd. But when you push for more popularity, your children get the message that something is wrong with them if they aren't part of what I call the charismatic kids. Also, if you emphasize popularity or being part of the clique, your children may become followers who go along blindly with the crowd.

Encourage quality over quantity. The number of friends your children have is less important than having one or two good friends. I know a dad whose eleven-year-old son has a couple of close friends but prefers not to socialize as much as his father thinks he should. This dad is constantly saying, "What are you doing this weekend? Why don't you call someone? Why don't you invite a bunch of kids over? I'll get pizza." I imagine the boy sees his father as disappointed that his son is not more popular.

If children are left out—or picked on by their peer group— help them recognize that it is not necessarily their fault. Reassure them that it is normal, though painful, to be "in" one week and "out" the next.

Sometimes these popularity contests can be more upsetting to parents than to kids. Many children are more resilient than we give them credit for. Try to ride the waves of friendship fads, remembering that young people are fickle and peer groups are constantly in a state of flux.

Don't Interfere Without Good Reason

Unless your children's friends are leading them into potentially hazardous situations, resist meddling in their relationships. If you suspect that risky behavior is involved, remind your children about your clear, firm rules. Tell them, "Safety is a nonnegotiable issue in this family."

Otherwise, allow children opportunities to negotiate their own issues and differences. Kids need time among themselves to learn how to develop their own rules, to share and take turns, to play fair, and to recover from bruised egos. Certainly there are times and places for adult supervision, but try to intervene only when necessary. Of course, you must step in if your child is constantly a victim or is repeatedly picked on, rejected, or humiliated.

A helpful resource for parents on bullying is a book by Charlene Giannetti and Margaret Sagarese titled *Cliques: 8 Steps to Help Your Child Survive the Social Jungle* (Broadway Books, 2001).

Listen to Your Child

The stronger children's self-confidence, the better they'll be able to resist negative influences of peers. Help strengthen children's egos by listening attentively when they're having trouble with friends.

Don't jump right in with ready-made solutions or criticism. Invite your child to tell you what happened but refrain from overreacting. They're not likely to open up if you go through the roof.

For example, your son comes home in tears because his friends ridiculed him for backing out of a scheme to shoplift. Don't yell, "You're not spending time with those kids ever again!" Instead, listen to his anguish about being ridiculed. Encourage him to talk about his feelings, and praise him for being strong and taking an unpopular stand.

You might say, "I know that was tough. I'm proud of you for not going along with them. I'm wondering, though, if these are kids you *really* enjoy being with."

Accept Their Right to Choose Friends

Keep in mind that you and your child have widely varying tastes and opinions. She may be attracted to people whom you don't relate to at all, just as you and she probably don't share the same tastes in food, music, or movies.

Try to respect your children's right to choose their friends even when their choices don't appeal to you. When your child mentions a new best friend, don't grill him with lots of intrusive questions. Withhold your judgment. Even if you don't like some of his friends, don't automatically denigrate them, especially without any evidence of harmful behavior. For many kids, the peers you disparage become all the more attractive.

76. Plan Successful Play Dates

Play dates give children a host of opportunities to learn new skills. From the preschooler's struggle with sharing to an older child's first experience practicing empathy and compassion, time with peers is an essential part of learning to get along in the world. However, play dates can also pose special problems. Rather than playing well together, kids often argue and fight, and your ears may be assaulted by the sound of your child or his friend shouting, "It's mine!" "Let go!" "I'm telling!"

Although you may want to intervene—and may need to before the arguments come to blows—you also want to avoid embarrassing your child or his friend. A dad whose nine-year-old son had a friend over was annoyed to hear them arguing heatedly. When they began to trade insults—"You're a jerk!" "Idiot!" and worse, he tried to decide whether to step in. Fortunately, he hesitated, because a few minutes later, they were quietly playing chess together. While we're busy worrying over their lack of social skills, kids move on. They're quick to forgive and forget. Adults can hold grudges for months, kids for minutes.

In fact, even when arguments erupt, play dates provide an invaluable chance for children to learn simple methods of conflict resolution. And while it can be tempting to try to solve children's problems for them, kids need to be encouraged to find their own solutions without too much adult intervention. So that they have a chance to learn to compromise, try asking, "How can you two work this out together?"

Encourage Sharing

Young children have a lot of trouble sharing their prized possessions—or anything else, for that matter. Although you can begin to talk to children as young as two about the concept of taking turns, it is wise to keep your expectations very low. Remember, they have only recently learned to say "mine," and it will take a while for them to learn how to say "yours" and, eventually, "ours."

Choose toys that are easy for young children to share, such as blocks, waterproof paint, or Play-Doh, and simple board or card games.

Be Clear About Rules

One of the stickiest challenges that parents face when they set up play dates is what to do when their rules conflict with those of another family. For instance, you might not allow your four-year-old to have cake, cookies, or candy except at parties but discover that on play dates with your neighbor, the girls can have all the cookies and candy they want. If you're not willing to compromise and your neighbor isn't cooperative, it might be better to have her child over to your house. However, decide what really matters to you and what is less important. Another parent may be extremely strict, while you are not. Conversely, you may find that other parents set almost no limits, forcing you to play the heavy when their children visit ("No, Ben, we only paint on paper at our house, not on walls!").

When a clash in rules or values occurs, your best move is to stick to your guns. It won't always be pleasant, and you may incur the wrath of your child, her friend, and her friend's parents. However, in the long run, it's easier than putting up with an anything-goes environment for play dates.

Avoid Unhappy Endings

It's very common for children to get upset when their play dates are over. If they've been having fun together, they hate for the visit to end. Also, many children have difficulty with transitions and saying good-bye. Ricky, five, had looked forward to visiting his friend Andrew's house all week, and they had spent a delightful afternoon together. When five o'clock rolled around and Ricky's father arrived to pick him up, the boy started to cry as soon as he heard his father's voice. He and Andrew scurried under the table to hide. When his dad appeared in the doorway, Ricky screamed, "Go home, Daddy!" Much resistance and many tears later, Dad finally got Ricky out the door.

To avoid a repeat performance, Ricky's dad thought of a creative solution. He asked Andrew's parents to prepare Ricky for his arrival. About fifteen minutes before the end of the date, Ricky was told that his father was on his way over and both kids had to start cleaning up. Kids almost never argue with the requests made by their friends' parents.

With planning, you can help your children's play dates go more smoothly and provide them with positive learning experiences.

77. Encourage the Grandparent Bond

In my grandmother's eyes, I could do no wrong. My mother's job was to raise me—to set limits, enforce rules, establish consequences, and teach me how to get along in the world. My grandmother's role was to admire and enjoy me with very few judgments or criticisms. To this day I remember how good it felt to be the recipient of her unconditional love and delight. She was such an important person in my life, and I still miss "Goggie."

I imagine that my mother wasn't always so pleased when her mother indulged, defended, and spoiled me. But somehow Mom knew to let the bond between us alone. When I became a parent myself, I realized that wasn't such an easy thing to do. As important as the grandparent-grandchild relationship is, our parents and in-laws can sometimes put us in an uncomfortable position with our children. They often disapprove of how we approach child rearing and may even be quite vocal about it. They might also overindulge our kids. Sometimes our own unresolved issues with Dad and Mom get in the way of our accepting their special bond with our children. There are many potential problems.

The question is, What can be done to help ease the strain and open the way for a mutually enriching relationship between your child and his grandparent? Let's look at a couple of common scenarios and how you might handle them more effectively.

Problem 1: When They Overindulge

Sometimes grandparents overindulge children with too many gifts because they don't know a better way to express their pleasure in a child. And grandparents do get enormous pleasure from buying things for their grandchildren. It's so much fun to watch a young child enthusiastically receiving a gift. In trying to form a tangible connection with their grandchild, they may feel that giving material things is one of the best ways to show their love.

If you're concerned that they're going overboard, you can help them establish their value in your child's life in different ways by reinforcing the message that what your child really needs is to be with them and to bask in their affection or undivided attention. For example, you might say sympathetically, "Oh, Mom, you don't have to bring Ellie a new toy every time you come. What she really loves and looks forward to is the time you spend with her at the playground."

Problem 2: When They Undermine Your Authority

Sometimes it seems as if your own parents are almost gleeful about undermining your authority. As one father observed ruefully, "It's like they've been waiting for the chance to get back at me for all my misdeeds when I was a kid, and now they have it." He described how when Grandpa and Grandma were around, the household rules went out the window. When he announced it was time for five-year-old Karen to go to bed, his mother would say, "Oh, it's still early. Let her stay up a little later." Or he'd catch Karen's grandfather being conspiratorial as he slipped her an illegal treat, overhearing him whisper, "Don't tell your daddy." He tried discussing his observations with his father but ran into nothing but protestations of innocence. "Who, *me?*" was his father's most common retort.

It's not unusual for people to feel as if they're engaged in a power struggle with their parents. Of course, it's frustrating when you've finally managed, after much effort, to establish a rule, only to have it treated lightly or ignored by the grandparents. In the previous instance, Grandpa seems to have no respect for his son's efforts to establish family rules.

Understand, too, that collusion sometimes creates a special bond. Nothing makes a child happier than thinking he's put one over on Mom or Dad. I think it's best to relax some of the rules a bit when the grandparents are around, while making it clear to your child that it's a special occasion. And accept the fact that when your children are at their grandparents' house, many of your rules will be ignored.

If you remember that your priority is to enable your children to develop close, lasting bonds with their grandparents, you'll probably be able to ease up somewhat. You may even have to get out of the way so that the relationship can develop on its own.

I'll never forget the mother who came to one of my workshops feeling very upset because her son was so taken with her father-in-law. "I can't stand him," she said, "I think his views on everything, from politics to religion, are ridiculous. But my son, who is nine, thinks he walks on water. He has no idea what a jerk his grandfather is." I immediately said, "For heaven's sake, don't tell him!"

The truth is, you don't have to personally like or approve of a grandparent in order for your child to get something special out of the relationship. No matter what his other flaws, this man seemed to be a very good grandfather. He was able to give a nine-year-old boy exactly what he needed at that moment and what he would cherish for the rest of his life: being loved unconditionally.

78. Teach Your Kids to Care

One of the greatest gifts a parent can give a child is a sense of compassion and caring about the world around her. In my experience, kids love to be engaged in helping others. They feel a true sense of self-worth when they know they've made a difference in another person's life.

So many parents these days complain about their children being too self-centered and materialistic. Perhaps the best way to challenge that is to make a point of being a family that cares.

There are many avenues available for children of all ages, as well as entire families, to help others in their local communities.

For example, a wonderful organization, Kids Care, offers hundreds of projects for kids in communities across America. Kids Care is based on the premise that the caring instinct is like a muscle; it needs to be developed. Your community, school, or church may already have a Kids Care Club, or you can start your own. Check out the website at www.kidscare.org.

However, you don't have to join an organization in order to get involved. Start small by making charity a part of your family life. Parents I know have tried some of these ideas for engaging their families and children in helping activities:

- Write or read letters for elderly patients in nursing homes.
- Contribute coats, sweaters, and blankets to places that distribute warm clothes to needy families.
- Visit elderly relatives or neighbors in your community. Have your child draw them a picture or share a favorite book.
- Volunteer to read stories or play games with hospitalized children.
- Bake cookies or treats for friends, neighbors, or relatives who live alone.
- Collect toys and books, and make lesson folders for classmates who have had to miss school because of illness.
- Clean up an empty lot or other community eyesore, or spend a few hours cleaning your local park or playground of any loose trash and weeds.
- Help an elderly or infirm neighbor with shopping and yard work.
- Recycle with your kids, and take them with you to the recycling collection center.
- Join a soup kitchen and volunteer on a regular basis.

Be sure to set aside time to talk about your experiences and to get your children's feedback. Some families write about these events and keep them in a special notebook. This notebook may end up being one of your family's most prized possessions. Modeling kindness yourself is the most powerful way to instill that virtue in your children since kids watch what we do much more than attending to what we say.

PART 9

![square]

Build Self-Esteem

79. Empower the Shy Child

Most parents wish their kids would adapt well to new situations and make friends easily. Instead, timid children will cling to our legs or hang on the sidelines. When they refuse to try an unfamiliar activity, we push them to participate. We become disappointed, annoyed, or frustrated with them when they aren't as outgoing as we'd like. How can we encourage our shy children, without pushing too hard?

- **Try a little understanding.** Remember how you felt when you walked into an office full of new coworkers or attended a party where you knew no one? Everyone gets anxious or self-conscious sometimes, but most adults find ways to deal with shyness because they've discovered that hanging back doesn't work for them. Children haven't yet learned how to cope with the unfamiliar, so they tend to feel even more ill at ease and awkward.

- **Recognize that your child doesn't *choose* to be shy.** Some researchers say that two out of five children are shy by nature. This temperamental trait is believed to be partly genetic. Some kids are born shy, just as they are born with brown eyes or curly hair. We can't reengineer this inborn characteristic, but we can help kids become more relaxed and adaptable.

- **Curb the criticism.** A shy child hears enough criticism—from herself and others. Whenever an adult pushes her ("Don't be so timid! Just try out for the school play. You'll never get a part if you don't make an effort."), she gets the message that there's something wrong with her for not participating. She probably hears her own inner voice carping, "I'm such a chicken for not trying out for that play." Children who are naturally reserved begin to believe this quality is a personal shortcoming. This further undermines their self-confidence and does little to encourage them to try new things or become more outgoing.

- **Avoid labeling.** When kids repeatedly hear, "He's always shy," or, "She's the bashful one in the family," their hesitancy about trying new things is only reinforced. Labeled shy, they continue to react that way and live up to that expectation. The label—like all labels—can also translate into negative descriptions, such as "awkward," "withdrawn," and "a wallflower," which are hardly confidence builders. Worse still, these labels can become self-fulfilling prophecies.

- **Build on strengths.** Reticent kids often have low self-esteem, particularly if they've been viewed as quiet and shy for a long time. They probably aren't the most popular kids at school. They tend to be the last child chosen by their peers for the team. Because they're reluctant to raise their hands in class, their intelligence may be underappreciated. But you know your child's strengths, and you can help boost his self-confidence and pride in himself by letting him know the special qualities you enjoy and admire in him.

Finally, keep in mind that a shy nature isn't a bad thing. Kids who are slow to warm up are less likely to take potentially dan-

---

■ **What *Not* to Say to a Shy Child**

"What are you so scared of?"

"Nothing ventured, nothing gained."

"You're such a scaredy cat."

"What are you waiting for?"

"Don't be a baby."

---

gerous risks. For instance, shy children are less likely to get in a car with a stranger. And shy four-year-olds tend to grow up to become more cautious teenagers who wait and size up a situation before engaging in risky activities with friends. Finally, shyness is a quality that many kids outgrow—especially with our support.

80. Create a Bug-Brag List

One of the most effective ways for parents to focus on the positive qualities of their kids is an exercise we use in my workshops, called "bug-brag lists." Here's how it's done.

Begin by writing down everything that bugs you about your child: "He always begs for one more minute or one more cookie." "He's never satisfied." "She won't get into the bathtub and then, once in, refuses to get out." "He embarrasses me by being loud and boisterous in public." "He can't keep his hands to himself." "She rolls her eyes and mimics me when I ask her to do her chores." "He's so stubborn."

Next, on a separate piece of paper, write down the qualities about your child you admire, enjoy, and appreciate: "She loves music, and we have such a good time singing and dancing to our favorite tapes." "He's very affectionate and loves to cuddle." "She's a caring leader in her group of friends."

Here are some actual bug-brag lists, provided by parents.

For a three-year-old boy:

Bug
- Dawdles at mealtimes and won't eat.
- Whines when he wants something.
- Wakes up at six in the morning, jumps on our bed, and won't stop talking.
- Throws things when he's mad.
- Often doesn't listen when spoken to.

Brag
- Fills our home with song and laughter and love.
- Likes to help me fold clothes and prepare food.
- Tells me to put on a happy face when I'm sad or mad.
- Is beautiful and sensitive.
- Has a great sense of humor and fun.
- Hugs my legs and looks up into my eyes and smiles.

For a five-year-old girl:

Bug
- She's clingy and whiny when tired.
- She yells, "Mommeee!" at the top of her voice whenever I'm in another room.
- She sucks her thumb loudly in public.
- She doesn't want to dress herself in the morning.
- She stomps her feet when she's mad or doesn't get her way.
- She tells me she hates me.
- She accuses me of loving her sister more than I love her.

Brag
- When I hurt myself, she immediately goes to kiss the spot.
- She loves to do puzzles with me.
- She's not discouraged by failed attempts.
- She says she wants to be a beautiful butterfly when she grows up.
- She protects her little sister in crowded elevators by wrapping her arms around her.
- She has this incredible belly laugh.

For an eleven-year-old girl:

Bug
- Her room is a mess. She leaves dirty clothes and wet towels on the floor.
- I have to ask her over and over to get to bed.
- She likes to wear outfits that are too adult and provocative for an eleven-year-old.
- She's either tying up the phone or hogging the computer, or both.
- She sulks when she has to spend time with the family, especially when we visit relatives.

Brag
- She loves school and usually gets A's and B's.
- She sings like an angel.
- She has a wicked sense of humor and can really make me laugh.
- She's committed to the environment and recycles everything.
- She has a mind of her own. She's a leader, not a follower.
- She's courageous—always eager to try something new.

Time and again, the parents in my groups who take the time to do this exercise talk about feeling so much more positive and loving, especially toward their more challenging child. I know a mother who, after completing her list, took it a step further. She said to her son, "You have so many special qualities. I don't always tell you, but look, I've made a whole list. Would you like to hear it?" It was a loving moment, and she noticed that her son was calmer and better behaved for the next few days. One dad who did the exercise put his positive observations in writing by buying a card and sending it in the mail to his nine-year-old son. The boy keeps it on his desk and reads it often.

81. Help Your Child Feel Special

In today's harried, hurry-up world, parents often think that "special" time with their kids involves a major investment of time or money. But it doesn't require a trip to Disney World to shower children with special time and attention.

Here's a more valuable and lasting recipe: Take small chunks of time. Add your undivided attention. Mix with pleasurable activities, and follow this recipe on an ongoing basis. Make it a regular part of your family's life and treat it as an important ritual. Pencil it in your weekly appointment calendar if that works best for you, but remember also to keep your eyes open for spontaneous, unplanned opportunities to spend five or ten minutes of focused time with your kids.

Special time also involves sharing a pleasurable activity or event. They aren't serious museum excursions that parents hope will broaden their child's exposure to art or history but that the child finds boring. They aren't structured activities geared to making your kids more productive or higher achievers. Doing math problems with your child for thirty minutes a night doesn't fall into the category of "special" time. As important as it is to monitor kids' schoolwork, that is a task, a responsibility, and a duty.

When our boys were young, we took them to Washington, D.C., for a long weekend. We wanted to introduce them to the important historical sites and monuments and give them an appreciation for our country. Weeks after our trip, I asked Eric what he liked best about the trip, expecting him to mention one of the well-known sites such as the Lincoln Memorial. He replied, "When we flew kites together on the lawn." So much for culture!

Here are some suggestions to make special time a regular part of your parent-child connection:

- **Stay focused on your child.** If the phone rings, let the answering machine take the message, or tell the caller you'll call her back later. A parent of a five-year-old usually picked up a ringing phone but decided to let it ring while she and her son were playing. Surprised, her son said, "Mom, the phone." She said, "I'm going to let it ring. This is more important." He glowed!

- **Avoid multitasking.** You may be great at juggling several things at once in the workplace, but your child won't feel you're really involved with him if you're loading the dishwasher or checking your E-mail while playing a game together.

- **Follow your child's lead** when choosing how to spend this special time. His interests may not be yours, but the event will mean more to him if it involves an activity that he likes. Also look for common interests that you and your children share.

If everyone enjoys food, for example, go out and try different cuisines at neighborhood restaurants or cook them up together in your own kitchen.

• **Try to plan ahead.** If you have an exceptionally busy week and limited time to spend with your child, let her know in advance. "I can take off from work early on Thursday. What would you like to do between five and six o'clock?" This way, you won't come home expecting "special time" when she has already planned to spend the afternoon with a friend. She may be torn between you and her friend and possibly end up feeling grumpy about the choice.

• **De-emphasize "quality time."** The concept of quality time is really a myth. When parents attempt to turn each moment into an occasion to teach or improve a child, they rarely reach those expectations—and the child rarely enjoys it. The emphasis should be on connection and fun. It may be as simple as a bike ride together, a walk in the garden to look for insects, or a stroll along the beach to collect shells. Or it may end on a silly note, like jumping in a pile of leaves together after raking the lawn. Special times don't have to be momentous events; the best ones are usually simple and mutually enjoyable.

• **Give each of your children exclusive time.** If you have more than one child, plan to spend some one-on-one time with each of them on a regular basis. This is difficult in busy households, but you could alternate evenings: one child gets twenty minutes alone with you every Monday and Wednesday, while another gets the same on Tuesday and Thursday. This plan allows each child to look forward to sharing special time alone with you, without a sibling vying for your attention. When you begin this routine, make this ground rule very clear: no interruptions during special time. The other child's turn will come, so he cannot burst in on his sibling's time alone with you.

What means the most to children of any age are those moments when they feel their parents are focused exclusively on them. These special times make children feel valued and important because parent and child share a real connection. Kids are at ease and happy because they are at the center of a loving parent's spotlight.

82. Raise an Emotionally Healthy Child

When I ask parents what they do to ensure that their children are physically healthy, they don't have much trouble giving me a list of practical strategies: getting regular doctor's checkups and vaccinations, preparing healthy meals, encouraging plenty of exercise, and so on. Emotional health, however, is harder to define and thus more elusive. You can't take a child's emotional temperature or easily diagnose his moods and feelings, yet all parents know that emotional health is every bit as crucial as physical health.

Raising an emotionally healthy child requires continuous effort and an appreciation of your child's temperament. Every child responds differently to conflicts and challenges. Some children are naturally easygoing, while others find it more difficult to negotiate life's everyday crises. The following guidelines will help you interact with your individual child according to his needs.

Distinguish Between Feelings and Behavior

There is no such thing as a wrong feeling. Feelings just *are*. At one time or another, everyone feels frustrated, disappointed, angry, confused, scared, jealous, or sad. When people make statements like "I could just kill her!" or "I hate you," we need to understand that they're letting off steam, not planning murder or rejecting us. However, parents often forget this when their children make such angry statements. Remember, feeling something isn't the same as doing it.

Example: Six-year-old Tommy was angry because his mother wouldn't let him ride his bike after dinner. Instead, she asked him to help wash the dishes. Tommy picked up a plate and cried, "I feel like throwing this stupid plate out the window!"

Tommy's mom could have responded to such a provocative statement as if he really were planning to throw the plate out the window. She might have exclaimed, "How could you even *think* of doing such a thing? What's gotten into you?"

A more positive response would be to understand that Tommy's feelings are different from his actions. Tommy's mom might have said, "I know you wish you didn't have to help me with the dishes. Wouldn't it be great if we never had to wash dishes ever again?" In this way, Mom could acknowledge the legitimacy of Tommy's feelings—which is often all children need to hear when they make dramatic statements. Even if Tommy remained angry, Mom was giving him permission to feel that way.

Be an Askable Parent

Kids of all ages need to know that it's safe to ask their parents any question and that they can go to them when they are troubled, confused, or even embarrassed. An askable parent can be trusted to respond to questions nonjudgmentally, without overreacting, expressing shock, or using the question as an opportunity to nag, threaten, lecture, or scold.

Twelve-year-old Sandra came to her mother and asked, "Let's say you saw somebody drinking beer at a party. What would you do?" Sandra's mom assumed this was not a hypothetical question since Sandra had been at a party with her friends the previous evening.

Sandra's question might have provoked an alarmed response from her mother. Her mother could have reacted negatively with words such as, "If I can't trust you not to go to parties where the kids are drinking, you'll just have to stay home from now on."

Instead of assuming blame or getting into a lecture mode (bound to produce instant resistance in preteens), Mom could elicit more information with a positive response such as, "That's an important question. What do you think the best way to handle it would be?"

You can always express your ideas and reinforce your values, but it's more helpful to hear your preteen's thoughts and reactions first. This is a difficult but important skill that I call listening to *hear* rather than listening to *answer*.

Jennifer, a mother of three kids, ages twelve, nine, and five, tells her children, " 'You can ask me anything. I won't get mad.' And they do—and I really don't get mad."

Acknowledge Your Child's Uniqueness

It's easy to forget that your child is not just a reflection of you—a "chip off the old block." He or she is a unique individual whose personality, temperament, interests, and abilities may be quite different from yours, and also different from those of his siblings.

For instance, eight-year-old Jill was a very reserved child who tended to be anxious in crowds and frightened of new situations. At the other extreme, her six-year-old sister, Carrie, was very outgoing and sociable and couldn't wait to spread her wings. On Jill's first day at a new school, she was weepy and nervous. She begged her mother to come in with her.

A negative response would be for Mom, thinking that Jill was too dependent and needed to get over her shyness, to say, "That's ridiculous. Look at your sister, Carrie. She loves going to school, and she's not afraid." This statement certainly wouldn't enable Jill to feel more confident. It would make her feel ashamed of her very real fears.

However, this mother understood that her two daughters have very different styles and personalities. Rather than comparing Jill to her more sociable younger sister, Mom might respond in a manner that respects Jill's special need for reassurance. In this context, she might say, "I'll bet lots of kids are nervous on the first day they start a new school. It's a very big step. Remember, I'll be waiting for you right outside at two-thirty on the dot."

Raising an emotionally healthy child is not so much about the big moments as it is about the everyday, minute-by-minute issues of daily life. The ordinary exchanges you have with your children are full of opportunities to show them that you have faith in them. This is how we reinforce the positive messages that form the building blocks of their emotional health.

83. Appreciate Your Challenging Child

All children are challenging in some way or at some stage. But what distinguishes a truly challenging child is that he is simply more of everything—more intense, more excitable, more stubborn, more talkative, more defiant, and more rambunctious. A challenging child makes extraordinary demands on families.

While some children bounce back quickly from disappointments, this child's feelings of upset will linger. While some children more readily accept the household rules, this child has more extreme reactions to everyday situations. He will never just go with the flow. He'll defy you or argue over the slightest thing. She'll throw a tantrum because you cut the bread into triangles instead of squares or gave her a different brand of peanut butter or laid out the red shirt instead of the blue—and she'll do it ten times a day, not just once.

A challenging child makes everything you do so much harder, and because of that, you might find yourself feeling exhausted, exasperated, and discouraged. Often, parents of challenging kids feel isolated, embarrassed, and full of self-blame. They wonder why their kids just can't be like other well-adjusted children. They question their abilities as parents and blame either the child, themselves, or both. They may also resent the fact that their "high-maintenance" child drains so much attention away from their other children.

If you have such a child, don't despair. The following suggestions may help you to see your child in a different light.

Ease Up on Yourself and Your Child

The biggest mistake made by parents of challenging children is to invest all their energy into trying to fit a square peg into a round hole. Parents often view themselves as sculptors of their children's temperaments, perceptions, and personalities. They believe, erroneously, that by trying harder and harder, and insisting over and over again, they will finally get their child to change and become more amenable. Life with children doesn't work that way. Rather, the goal is to accept our children as they are, not the way we wish they were.

Kids mirror our attitudes toward them. Once a child gets the reputation for being "difficult," he'll behave accordingly. When we reflect back to a child that he's a pain, he continues to behave that way. But when we mirror the pleasure he gives us, he will often rise to the occasion. Nurtured with love, even the most challenging child can flourish.

It's easy to get emotionally and physically overwhelmed by the negatives—to the point where you're no longer able to see anything redeeming in your child. One mom admitted to me that even when her seven-year-old is full of exuberance, she's still dreading the moment it will turn into wild, unrestrained acting

---

■ Parent's Story: A Bright Light

From infancy, Sandra, the youngest of three, has been a bundle of energy, intensity, and willfulness. At first, Julia, her mother, was terribly frustrated by Sandra's unpredictable moods and behavior. She never knew when a mundane mishap—a few drops of juice spilled on the floor—would trigger loud shrieks or whether Sandra would suddenly feel a desperate need to remove her clothes in the middle of the grocery store. Everything took longer with Sandra. A trip from the front door to the car could turn into a ten-minute ordeal if she got absorbed in watching a bug.

Raising a "challenging" child like Sandra takes extra time, patience, and work. But Julia learned early on that Sandra's high-spiritedness is only as big a problem as Julia perceives it to be. Part of the way Julia keeps her perspective—especially on tough days—is by focusing on the positive qualities of her exceptional daughter. These positive traits are shared by many challenging children: "Sandra is perceptive, she's independent, she's a leader, and she's full of life," says Julia. "She can light up a room. People rarely talk about this side of raising a high-spirited child. They focus on the difficulties. They don't see what a tremendous gift it is to have a child like Sandra."

---

out. I can empathize. In fact, one of the reasons I became a parent educator is because I had to un-learn so much of what came naturally but that was detrimental to my kids' self-esteem. Had my children been the easy, happy, well-adjusted people I was anticipating, I would've been a wonderful mother. They were not. Instead of being more accepting and focusing on my sons' strengths, I overreacted to their irritating behavior. I regret the many times I said angrily, "What is the matter with you?"—a reaction that just reinforced the problem. How I wish I had known then what I know now—and what I've been trying to teach parents for the last twenty-five years.

Eight Great Traits of Challenging Children

The first step in seeing our children in a more positive light is to become aware of how our criticism is backfiring. Many challenging children grow into remarkable adults. As they gain independence, these kids discover new outlets for their passion and better ways of handling frustration. Then it's easier to see the positive traits that were there all along:

- **They are leaders.** They're not content to sit back and let others tell them what to do.
- **They march to a different drummer.** They're unique and have an original take on life.
- **They are intense and passionate.** They're able to feel emotions deeply and are often exceptionally creative.
- **They are unforgettable.** People notice them; they don't just fade into the woodwork.
- **They are independent thinkers.** They demand answers and search for reasons and meaning. They question the status quo.
- **They have high energy.** They won't sit in a stupor, vegging out in front of the TV. Passivity is not in their nature.

- **They usually know what they want.** They're not wishy-washy. When they want something, they want it with every inch of their being.
- **They are emotionally demonstrative.** Their expressions of love are spontaneous and sincere.

84. Encourage Perseverance

"Don't be such a quitter!" Many parents are annoyed and frustrated when they plunk down money for art classes, ballet, karate lessons, or other programs only to have their child drop out after two weeks. They feel as if they've just thrown their money away, and worse still, they don't like to think of their child as being a quitter. But it's a mistake to equate quitting with failure. Children have a healthy desire to experiment. They tend to be dabblers, eager to try different things, and their interest can fade quickly as they move on to the next project. It's a perfectly natural and positive way for them to gain exposure to a variety of activities before choosing those that they're willing to commit to.

The following suggestions will help you take a different view of quitting—and know how to evaluate when it's OK, when it's a problem, and how to respond:

- **Don't confuse your passion with your child's.** Sometimes a parent might be much more eager for a child to engage in an activity than the child is himself. We all know about those enthusiastic parents who want their kids to excel at the piano or other musical instrument. How many of those instruments are now gathering dust in back rooms and attics? Perhaps you love tennis, so you urge your child to try it, then are disappointed when he quits, not appreciating the fact that he never had a real desire to play tennis in the first place. Listen to what your child wants, not just what *you* want.

- **Don't make it do-or-die.** Before making a commitment, let your child observe a class in session. Or ask the teacher if she'll let him try it out once or twice to see if he likes it before you sign up. Most teachers will be happy to oblige. Also, find out in advance what is required. How much practice will there be? How many hours a week? Often children quit because they never understood the extent of the commitment they were making.

- **Do encourage your child to try again if he gets discouraged.** Maybe the problem is that he expects to be perfect the first time he tries something and is impatient with the trial and error that goes into learning a skill. He might think karate looks like fun when he sees Bruce Lee snapping out kicks on TV but be bored by the grueling nature of a real karate class. Help your child understand the process of mastery. Learning takes time and practice.

- **Do try to find out why she wants to quit.** If your child announces that she wants to quit a project she was once excited about, find out the reason. Maybe there's an external problem you can address—like a bully in the group or a teacher who may be ignoring your child. Or, if the problem is internal, such as a lack of self-confidence, you can offer support and encouragement.

- **Do check out the teacher or coach.** Try to find someone who not only is an expert at the activity she's teaching but also enjoys and understands kids. Without that combination, it will be much more difficult to motivate your child. When one of my sons wanted to take piano lessons, I was lucky to find a teacher who not only excelled at the piano but also really loved kids. Her warmth and enthusiasm made all the difference.

- **Do look for progress, not perfection.** Sometimes a child quits because his vision is so different from reality. He thinks he has to be perfect right away. Offer praise for small accomplishments. For example, if your child is learning to ice-skate, measure success by her ability to go around the rink without falling, then move on to the next level. Teach your child that satisfaction can be experienced in the process of learning, not just in the final result.

- **Don't forget that the goal of sports, classes, and activities is not just educational.** You want your child to have fun. No child is going to want to stick with a project if the fun is missing.

85. Help Your Child Be a Good Loser

Being a good sport—learning how to lose—is an essential social skill. But it's hard to teach your child the value of sportsmanship if you yourself react to losing with anger or disappointment. In recent years, there have been many incidents of "parent rage" at kids' sporting events. These incidents have resulted in physical injury and, in one shocking case, the death of a parent, for which the attacker (another parent) is currently serving a prison sentence. Since our children get most of their cues about how to behave from their parents, it's essential that we model sportsmanlike behavior ourselves. Many parents volunteer as coaches and send positive messages to the kids they coach, including their own children.

Learning how to lose gracefully is a key factor in getting along in the world. Research shows that bad losers have more trouble than other children in making and keeping friends. The primary reasons children get involved in sports are to expand their social networks, participate in organized play, get exercise, and learn teamwork. Being a sore loser undermines these goals.

Here are some ways you can help your child be a good loser:

- **Don't let him win all the time.** For example, kids love to beat their parents at games, and parents often let them win because it's much more fun to see their joy than their disappointment. However, if you let them win all the time at home, they may expect to win whenever they play games with their friends, too.

- **Praise the effort, not just the result.** Let your child know you're proud of her hard work and skills. Don't reserve your praise for when she wins. Watch what you say after a loss. Statements such as "Well, you sure weren't at your best today" or "Why weren't you concentrating better?" communicate your disappointment in her. Instead, you might say, "I always enjoy watching you play," or, "Well, today the other team won, but I admired your fighting spirit."

- **Talk about persistence and courage.** Make a conscious effort to point out examples of people who strive against all odds. For example, watching a baseball game, you might say,

"I admire the way that team never lets up, even though they're behind by so many runs." Or when your favorite skater falls during a competition, point out how she gets back up and keeps going with a smile, even though she's lost all hope of winning. Read books or watch movies about people who overcame adversity.

Finally, focus on the fun of playing. Games and sports, after all, are supposed to be fun. Win or lose, they create memories to be cherished for a lifetime. And a person who knows how to lose with grace and cheer is a person bound to be a winner in life.

■ Parent's Story: A Winning Strategy

"My son Robert, six and a half, loves to play board games. He also loves to be the winner. One day we were playing Monopoly, and he lost. He was so mad that he knocked the board to the floor.

"I told him I know he likes to win; everyone likes to win. But I wanted him to understand the importance of being a good sport. I gave him two options: one, continue to play, but if he loses and can't control his temper I'd stop playing with him for a week or two; or two, stop playing altogether until he feels he can control his temper and be a good sport when he loses."

---

86. Let Kids Be Kids

We have friends who treat their only child like a small adult. Henry accompanies his parents everywhere and is included in many of their adult conversations. He's a very bright child, who attends a school for gifted students, but there's something sad about this child. He's so busy trying to be mature that he doesn't have much chance to be a kid. I've never seen him behave in a silly or spontaneous manner.

This sometimes happens not just with only children but when parents forget that one of the main benefits of having kids is to enjoy them. The idea of fun doesn't even enter into the mix.

Here are some tips for helping your kids be kids, not just miniature adults:

- Don't assume that your child is mature because she has more adult language skills than some of her peers. Often, adult matters need to be discussed out of a child's earshot. To establish such boundaries, you could say, "Daddy and I have to talk alone now." Also, avoid confiding adult worries or grievances to your child. Resist the temptation to make her your buddy.

- Let your children know that you and your spouse are a couple, not just their parents. Show them that your relationship is special in its own way. Send the message that just the two of you value time spent together. The best way to do this is to schedule regular time with your spouse apart from your children. I know of parents who are convinced that they have to take their children with them wherever they go—sometimes ignoring the fact that they're not always welcomed by other adults at restaurants, theaters, and dinner parties.

- All parents want their children to excel, but sometimes children feel uncomfortable in the spotlight of your hopes and dreams. Avoid trying to micromanage your children's everyday activities to prepare them for the future careers *you* imagine for them. Fight the temptation to express disappointment when your children have likes and dislikes that are different from your own. Instead, encourage them to discover their own interests and abilities.

Beware of the tendency to enroll your child in every activity imaginable, from skating instruction to gymnastics classes to piano lessons to studying French—the list is endless. Children whose parents keep them occupied every minute never get the chance to know what it's like to just do nothing.

Dr. Alvin Rosenfeld, a friend and author of *The Over-Scheduled Child* (Griffin Trade Paperback, 2001), tells parents how to avoid the "hyper-parenting" trap. One of my favorite suggestions is "Be unproductive: A life that consists of endless activities demonstrates to our children that . . . they need to work hard at polishing and perfecting themselves, and says implicitly that we don't believe they are good enough as they are." Encourage your children to develop relationships with kids their own age and participate in unstructured activities. Let them relish the child's world they live in for as long as it lasts. There will be plenty of time for serious adult matters later, but kids get only one chance to be kids.

87. Send Valentines Throughout the Year

A mother in one of my workshops shared this Valentine's Day letter she sent to her son:

Dear Myles,

Happy Valentine's Day to my dearly beloved son. There are so many things about you that give me joy—your laugh and sweet smile, your generous and caring nature, the way you help me see that we can always recover our good feelings for each other, no matter how mad we've gotten. I also delight in your sense of humor and your truly original way of looking at the world and its inhabitants.

I am so happy and grateful that you are a part of my life. Valentine's Day is a good excuse to remind you how much I love you.

Lots of love,
Mom

I found this letter quite touching. How wonderful to be the recipient of such a loving message. It occurred to me, however, that too often we assume our kids know we love and appreciate them, and we don't take the time to point out the specific ways they're special.

Wouldn't it be wonderful if we made an effort to send our kids the equivalent of a written or verbal valentine—not just on February 14, but throughout the year? One way we can do this is to practice what I call "One-a-Day Esteem Builders." Find at least one opportunity during the course of each day to tell your child she's a source of pride and joy to you, just as she is. The key is to be specific. Here are some examples:

"Your jokes are so funny. Someday you might be a stand-up comedian."
"Look at the way your baby brother tries to imitate you!"
"Wow! How did you manage to put that toy together? I couldn't even figure out the directions."
"You should see the way Spot's face lights up when he hears you coming in the door."
"I appreciate the way you kept a protective eye on your little sister in that crowded department store."

From these small, seemingly insignificant statements, self-esteem grows and flourishes.

PART 10

■

Strengthen Parenting Skills

88. Drop the Perfect-Parent Fantasy

Every day, mothers and fathers are bombarded by input about what it means to be a good parent. Magazines are full of advice. Some of us were raised watching television programs that showed loving parents living in happy harmony with their children, enjoying uplifting conversations around the dinner table. Those images stuck. Child psychologists appear on talk shows to preach the latest rules of good parenting. Often this barrage of images and input leaves parents feeling guilty. They're afraid they'll never measure up to the ideals of parenthood. On the other hand, the media is also full of stories about people who grew up in so-called dysfunctional families and were scarred for life. It's no wonder that some parents fear that no matter what they do, they'll never measure up. Writer Fay Weldon said it best: "The great advantage of *not* having children is you're able to hold on to the idea of what a great person you are."

The truth is, the ideal family doesn't exist. It's time for parents to stop feeling guilty when they can't meet these impossible standards. And there's a huge difference between how we imagine we will be as parents and how we actually are. I can't count the number of times I've heard a parent say, "I vowed I'd be totally different from my parents and yet end up doing the exact same things!"

Let's explode some of the most damaging myths.

Myth: Good parents love all of their children equally.
Any adult with siblings knows from experience that children within a family are treated differently. It makes sense when you consider that each child is a unique personality. But parents drive themselves crazy trying to apportion their love and attention in exactly equal amounts. Although we try as parents not to play favorites, it's inevitable that we're going to sometimes prefer one child to another, especially when that child is easier to deal with.

Myth: If you work at it, you can achieve "quality time" with your children.
The myth of quality time is hard on parents. First of all, nobody ever defined quality time, so parents feel guilty that they aren't achieving it. Second, kids aren't always so cooperative about going along with your best-laid plans for time together. The myth of quality time destroys the spontaneity of enjoying life with your children in everyday ways. It puts you and your children under unnecessary pressure to meet some impossible ideal.

Myth: You and your kids can agree about what's fair.
The most frequent complaint of siblings is "It's not fair." (They'll count the number of M&M's in a bag to make sure one isn't getting more than the other!) So, no matter how equally we try to treat them, they'll never agree that we're being fair. One parent told me her kids counted the number of photos their parents took on vacation to see which child appeared in the most pictures. Parents would do better to accept the inevitability of this eternal complaint and just go with the flow. It's a waste of your precious time to try to convince siblings that life is fair.

Myth: If you love your kids, they'll be grateful and love you back.
Many parents have trouble saying no or setting limits because they worry about the temporary unhappiness this creates in their children. But part of a parent's job is to be the party pooper of their kids' lives. Although we make endless sacrifices for our children, they're not always going to show their gratitude—especially when we most expect them to. As the late parenting guru Dr. Haim Ginott so eloquently said, "The tragedy of parenthood is that we are their friends and they don't know it, and they are not our friends and we don't know it."

The fantasy that we can be perfect parents raising perfect families only creates guilt, self-reproach, and regret. The "good enough" parent is a worthwhile and more realistic goal—and that probably describes you if you're reading this book!

89. Don't Let Your Kids Divide and Conquer

The "united front" is an unrealistic goal when raising children. It's normal for parents to disagree occasionally about discipline. After all, Mom and Dad aren't joined at the hip. Each has individual temperaments, preferences, and priorities—not to mention different upbringings. However, most kids have a flawless instinct for recognizing division in the ranks and using it to their advantage. If you and your spouse have an obvious difference of opinion about a rule or method of discipline, your children are going to pick up on it and use that division to their advantage.

So how can you work as a team to set clear, consistent standards for your kids? How can you avoid sending mixed messages or letting them play one of you against the other? The key is to strive for common ground and compromise rather than a false united front. Here are some guidelines:

- **Accept and respect your differences.** Each of you had a different set of parents. Your spouse may have grown up in a laid-back family with few rules, while your parents may have been very strict. Whether we replicate or reject our own parents' disciplinary methods, our childhood experiences will influence the way we raise our own kids today. In fact, our parents were our only teachers, and many of us feel we need a different model for raising our own kids.

- **Agree to disagree—but in private.** When your spouse handles a disciplinary problem in a way you don't approve, bite your tongue for the moment. Don't contradict or undermine your spouse by disagreeing in front of your child. Later on, you can say something like, "I know Billy's behavior really got to you. He can be very challenging. I wonder if another approach might work better. What do you think?"

- **Avoid falling for the divide-and-conquer game** that kids play so well (otherwise known as "If Mom says no, go to Dad for a yes"). Establish this clear rule: when one parent says no, it's no. Make certain your kids understand this rule; remind them of it, and enforce it when they break it. Parents can't agree on every rule, but they need to agree on the "big" ones. In one family, the first parent to discover that a rule has been broken may want to decide the consequences, and he needs to be backed up by the other parent.

- **Stay out of the middle.** When your child pleads with you to intervene in a conflict he has with your spouse, don't jump into the fray. Simply say, "That's between you and your mom. I think you can work it out." Encourage your child to discuss the situation directly with the other parent. (This is important in all families, but it's especially crucial when parents are divorced or the child lives in a blended family.) Remember that kids often try to play one parent against the other in the hope that the resulting conflict will divert your attention and they'll get what they want.

- **Buy some time.** When your child has a disagreement or complaint about the other parent and you're caught unaware of the details, you don't have to respond with an instant opinion or verdict. Instead, you could say, "Mom and I will talk this over and get back to you." This is a useful response when your child makes a request that you think you and your spouse

---

■ Parent's Story: Don't Tell Dad

Elinor, a parent in my workshop, told about the time her ten-year-old daughter got a C-minus on a math test and pleaded, "Mom, please don't tell Dad. He'll really be mad!" It was true that Elinor's husband got much more upset about less-than-stellar grades. But Elinor replied, "Janie, either you can tell him, or I will. We don't keep secrets from each other." However, when Elinor and her husband were alone, she did tell him that his daughter was very scared of his reaction so that he could temper his response and not fly off the handle when Janie told him the unpleasant news.

---

may have different opinions about. And with older children, you can explain that you and your spouse might not always agree: "As you know, Mom and I don't feel the same way about every issue." Then talk with each other and see if you can reach a workable compromise.

- **When you do argue, fight fair.** Try as you might to work as a team, it's inevitable that at times you and your spouse will openly disagree. When that happens, it's important to avoid name-calling and sarcasm. As you feel your anger rising, take some time to cool off and revisit the problem later. Don't attack your spouse with blame, as in, "You always let her get away with bloody murder," or, "You never back me up," or, "Why do you always have to make me the bad guy?" Instead, state how you feel: "I get angry when the kids see me as the mean mom and you as the good guy."

■ Parent's Story: A Different Approach

In my workshop, one mother complained frequently about the way her husband expressed his anger at their two-year-old daughter. She was continuously reproaching him, admonishing him to stop barking and act more gently toward their little girl. Her complaints only made him defensive. He'd usually react by criticizing his wife: "Well, someone has to discipline her. You're too soft with her." After discussing the problem with the other parents, this mother was able to approach her husband more diplomatically: "I guess sometimes I am too easygoing—maybe that's why she ignores me. But I'd like you to watch her face when you yell at her. She looks very scared of you. You're very big and she's very small. I know you want her to feel safe with you, and you're the most important man in her life."

When children have seen the two of you fighting about disciplinary issues, be sure to let them know that although you disagree, you still respect each other. Once you've cooled off, it's helpful for the kids to see that you're able to make up.

When you do have an argument, reassure your kids that it's not their fault. Show them that even when adults disagree, they still love each other. Children can understand and accept different parenting styles. In fact, it helps them learn about the range of human emotions and demonstrates the art of compromise and problem solving.

90. Ignore Your Critics

When you become a parent, you soon discover that everyone is an expert. Family members, friends, and even complete strangers don't hesitate to offer unsolicited advice or criticism.

When my children were young, I was flooded with advice, as if everyone else knew much more about proper child raising than I did. I was also surrounded by innumerable critics—from the stranger in the supermarket who asked why I couldn't keep my kids in line to my childless adult friends who were dismayed by my children's imperfect table manners. Then, of course, I had parents and in-laws who often frowned upon my various approaches to discipline. It never occurred to me that I could just ignore them. Instead, I took every criticism to heart, letting it further reinforce my feelings of inadequacy.

Looking back on those days, I wish I had been secure enough to recognize that I often *did* know better what was best for my children. I wish I hadn't cared so much about the remarks, stares, and blatant disapproval of complete strangers. When my childless friends lectured me about parenting, I wish I had smiled and remembered the adage, "Those without children always know best how to bring up yours."

Snappy Comebacks for Busybodies

Perfect strangers also seem to be just loaded with "good advice." Of course, you can always ignore them. But parents have told me they resent the criticism and long for a good—and civil—comeback. One day I asked my workshop group to think of possible responses to be used when a stranger puts his or her two cents in. They had some great ideas:

- To the man who says, "Your son is obnoxious": Reply coolly, "I'm sorry you feel that way," and turn your back.

- To the woman who comments loudly, "How can she let her child go out in public looking like that?": Laugh and say, "I think she looks fabulous in sequins."

- To the man who teases your daughter by saying, "Hey, little girl. Cat got your tongue?": State firmly, "My daughter has been taught not to talk to strangers."

- To the woman who openly criticizes the way you handle your child: Say, "I'm sure you'd do it differently if *you* were his mother."

- To the man who says, "In my day we didn't let kids get away with that": Ignore him—and work on perfecting your steely "Clint Eastwood" stare.

91. Lessen Parent Guilt

Before my children were born, I was convinced that I would be patient, kind, and nurturing—the quintessential earth mother. But I failed to live up to the ideal mother image that I had pictured for myself. I was daunted by the enormous gulf between the perfect parent that I wanted to be and the flawed parent that I actually was. Since then, I have learned that such feelings are quite common. Scratch any parent, and you'll find guilt. It's lurking just beneath the surface, ready to spring out when we lose patience with our children, fail to make them happy, feel resentful of their demands, or believe that when they misbehave it's all our fault.

Most parental guilt is unproductive. It is a fatiguing repetition that leads to self-accusation, not action or change. If you suffer guilt pangs when your expectations and reality don't match, practice learning to minimize the guilt. Recognize instead all the ways in which you are doing well as a parent. Parents have admitted to me that they were glad they didn't know in advance how exhausting and demanding a job it would be to have kids. Although few, if any, regret the challenge, many wish they could have time off. One mom said, "Wouldn't it be great if I could use the remote control to put her on mute?!"

Here are typical guilt triggers.

"I'll Make It Up to Him" Guilt

Every morning, after Alena dropped off her three-year-old son, Brian, at preschool, she felt terribly guilty. Alena had recently returned to work full-time, and Brian now spent his mornings at a nursery school in their neighborhood and his afternoons with his grandmother. Every morning he wailed, "Mommy! Come back!" when she left him, and his parting cries haunted Alena all day. To make matters worse, the pressure of learning her new job left Alena exhausted in the evenings. She no longer had the energy to play hide-and-seek or tag. Now she just wanted to hold Brian on her lap and read to him or curl up, semi-comatose, on the couch, watching a video with him.

Although Brian's teacher assured Alena he calmed down quickly once she left, she couldn't let herself off the hook. So after a few weeks of wrenching, tearful good-byes, Alena arranged to leave work early one Friday to surprise Brian. She had planned a great afternoon—a trip to the pizza parlor followed by a couple of hours at the zoo. But to her surprise, Brian wasn't thrilled to see her when she arrived early to pick him up. "Grandma always takes me to the playground after school," he complained, "I don't want to leave yet."

Because she felt guilty, Alena put a lot of pressure, both on herself and on Brian, to have that "perfect" afternoon that would make up for her not being as available as she had been before. When the day didn't go exactly as she had planned, Alena felt as if she had somehow failed Brian.

"Mean Mommy" Guilt

All parents want their children to be happy. But sometimes this desire conflicts with the need to set limits. Unfortunately, when you say no, your kids are hardly going to compliment you on your good judgment. Many parents feel terrible when their children express anger or make accusations. I like the response of a mother in my workshop, when her five-year-old screamed, "Mommy, I hate you! You're mean."

"Well, sweetie," she smiled, "sometimes the *M* in *mommy* stands for *mean*." This mother of three doesn't let her kids push her guilt buttons.

"I Should" Guilt

Many of us are plagued by "shoulds": You "should" serve a hot meal every night. You "should" send your kids to school in clothes that match. You "should" take your children to the park on a nice day. You "should" make sure they watch only educational TV. But sometimes the best move is to forget the shoulds and ease up on ourselves. Albert Ellis, the founder of Rational Emotive Behavior Therapy, once said, "Thou shalt not should on thyself." To the extent that we reject the tyranny of guilt, we can be freer to enjoy time with our children.

I can still remember an incident that happened when my sons were young. It was a snowy day, and the schools were closed. I tried to get the boys excited about going outside. But it was very cold, and they wanted to stay indoors. I was about to say, "What a waste staying home! We should build a snowman or go sledding!" Suddenly, though, I realized that it didn't really matter whether we stayed indoors. And frankly, I myself hate cold weather. So we stayed in our pajamas the entire day, drank hot chocolate, played games, and had a wonderful time. It felt so good, for once, to let go of the shoulds and wave good-bye—however briefly—to guilt.

Guilt-Busting Responses

Most kids learn early on how to push their parents' guilt buttons. Guilt is a powerful motivator for parents' tendency to overindulge their children. It's hard to see your child's eyes welling up with tears and that lower lip starting to quiver and not feel like a mean parent—especially if your child adds the appropriate guilt-producing punch line. Following are some typical remarks children blurt out when they want their way—and the guilt-busting responses you might try.

YOUR CHILD SAYS . . .	YOU CAN RESPOND . . .
"I'm never going to be your friend."	"Oh, I hope you change your mind because I was looking forward to reading with you before bedtime."
"Daddy's nice, but you're mean!"	"I know you don't like it when I say no."
"I hate you."	"Wow! I can see you're really angry."
"You don't love me."	"Honey, we're not talking about love. We're talking about a nice, hot bath that is waiting for you to get in."
"You *always* say no."	"Well, I guess that's my job."
"I'm running away."	"Oh, that would make me too sad. I won't let you go."
"You love her more than me."	"Is that what you think? How about an extra big hug?"
"I wish you weren't my mommy."	"I bet you wish you could go to the Mommy Store and pick out a different one."

92. Share the Parenting with Dad

Since more than 80 percent of all mothers work outside the home at least part-time and 52 percent of them have children under age one, being a parent has become more stressful than ever. Often, the sheer uphill battle of each day—getting the kids up and to school, racing to work, hurrying home to messy houses and piles of laundry and dinner to be cooked—demoralizes mothers completely. There's never a break. Many mothers complain that they're not getting the help they need from their spouses. Although more fathers than ever before are very involved with their children, many moms complain that most of the parenting burden still falls on them.

Often, however, moms don't recognize their own complicity in maintaining the status quo. For example, a frequent complaint that comes up in my workshops is what I call the Let–Get Syndrome: "How do I *get* my husband to . . . ," or, "Should I *let* my husband . . . ." Women want their spouses to help out more, but they don't always see how they sabotage men's efforts to be equal partners by insisting that everything be done on their own terms. One mother laughingly recalled that she was so exhausted at the end of one day, she yelled at her husband, "I've had it! *You* take over." She stormed upstairs but was back in five minutes, asking why their daughter wasn't in her pajamas yet and expressing disapproval at the TV program she was watching. She admitted, "I told him to take over, but I really meant, 'Take over and do it my way.'"

Most fathers want—and need—to play an important role in their children's everyday lives, but they're less apt to participate fully if they feel as if you're watching them like a hawk, ready to jump in with criticisms and complaints. In discussing this—a frequent topic in the workshop—one mother said, "There's one right way. Mine!" She said it jokingly, but we recognized it as serious kidding. Equal parenting is possible only if the mother is willing to relinquish her role as sole expert and voice of authority.

Here are some ways parents can enhance the father's role:

- **Work out together which of you will be responsible for certain daily tasks.** Even if the father has a very busy work schedule, it's important that he take over as many daily routines as possible—whether it's bath and story time, fixing breakfast, or taking the kids to school.

- **Bite your tongue when you are tempted to criticize**—or, better still, leave the room. Let Dad diaper the baby or fix a meal for the kids without worrying that he won't do it exactly the way you do.

- **Don't discourage fun time with Dad.** Many mothers complain that they are the heavies and their spouses are the playmates—a division that seems unfair. While dads need to be more to their children than playmates, the fun is important, too. Sometimes Mom needs to lighten up.

- **Fight fair.** When you disagree with your husband on child-raising issues, don't humiliate him or make him look inept in front of the children. You can disagree without assuming an "I know best" posture.

In the past, too many books, articles, and workshops focused solely on mothers and left out dads, as though they were less important. Fortunately, this is changing, as our awareness of the crucial role fathers play in influencing their children's sense of competence and self-esteem has grown. Dads *do* parent differently from moms, but it's the combination of their differences that enriches the family.

93. Make an Uninterrupted Phone Call

Children of all ages are drawn to the telephone as if it were a high-powered magnet. As soon as you get on the phone, it seems as if your formerly contented child needs you desperately. The phone rings, and suddenly siblings who were peacefully playing launch into full-fledged combat. Even your adolescent, who barely speaks to you, sees you're on the phone and *must* talk to you about something urgent immediately. As soon as you begin a phone conversation, you become an irresistible attraction.

Why do children see the phone as a rival? Because it is! Young children, especially, are self-absorbed, and they want you to be absorbed with them. They can't stand to see you spending "quality" time with anyone or anything that cuts in on their claims to your undivided attention.

If you've lost hope of ever having an uninterrupted phone call until your kids have left for college, here are some strategies to help your child cope with your busy signal and help you reclaim some pleasurable phone time:

- **Be prepared.** For young children, set aside a special selection of toys, drawing materials, or books that your child can take out only when you are on the phone. Toddlers, in particular, enjoy a toy phone. You can refresh the supply of toys every now and then, but if you manage to keep these items exclusively for phone time, their appeal will last longer.

- **Sometimes give your child top priority.** Let your child hear you occasionally tell friends that you'll call them back later. What a gift for your child to hear you say, "I can't talk to you just now. Matt and I are making a fort." He can only conclude that he's interesting and important to you.

- **Set a timer.** By setting a kitchen timer for ten or twenty minutes, you can show your child that your phone call is not going to last forever. Say to him, "I need you to wait until the timer rings. When it does, you come and tell me and I will end the call just as soon as I can."

- **Schedule your calls.** Limit your longer calls to times when your child is asleep. For example, tell friends that you can talk in peace during your child's nap time or after 8:00 P.M.

- **Take advantage of your answering machine.** It's a wonderful device for fending off unwanted interruptions. By letting the machine pick up messages, you can take the important calls and put off the ones that can wait.

You may still have to postpone that long chat with your college roommate until your child is in bed for the night, but at least during the day, you will be able to communicate with the outside world from time to time. And your child will eventually come to realize that the telephone is not the rival she once thought it was. Now, if only there were a way to encourage children to give their parents five minutes of peace to go to the bathroom alone!

94. Keep the Peace with Your Parents

There's a saying that grandparents and grandchildren get along so well because they have a common enemy—*you*! Many harried parents can attest to the truth of that statement. If you have control issues with your parents, these issues aren't necessarily going to disappear when you have a child of your own. If you and your parents don't see eye to eye on things—from how you live to what you believe—you can bet there's going to be discord once there are kids in the picture.

Here are some suggestions for minimizing the discord.

When Your Parent Criticizes You

Some people are just critical—and if your parents are among them, you're probably going to have limited success in changing that behavior. It's best to try to ignore them or to respond with a noncommittal, "Uh-huh," to their advice. And if you *do* have a critical parent on your hands, you might also consider the possibility that she isn't aware of the effect she's having on you. Believe it or not, she may just be trying to be helpful!

Maybe, too, she really does have some good advice to offer at times, but you reject it out of hand because you resent her involvement. Everyone likes to feel needed and appreciated, and a mother is no different. An effective strategy might be to occasionally ask for her advice before she spontaneously offers it. Or you might try a technique that a parent in one of my workshops used with great success. Whenever her mother criticized her about food or health issues, she simply said, "My pediatrician gave me these instructions." Case closed.

When Your Parent Disapproves of Your Children

The ideal relationship between a grandparent and a grandchild is one of unconditional love. When you see your parent being critical of your child, it can really hurt. Try approaching your mother or father in a nonconfrontational manner. I suggested this approach to a parent whose father expressed disapproval of her son's choice of clothing. "He may have never stopped to consider how much his opinion means to your son," I said. "You might say to him, 'Dad, I know it bugs you when Billy wears those baggy pants to school, but it really hurts his feelings when you make cracks about them. He cares deeply about your opinion.' At the same time, quietly stand up for your son, saying, 'It's OK with me if he dresses like that. He's a good student, and that's what really matters.'" You might also encourage your child to express his hurt feelings directly to the grandparent, without your acting as a go-between.

When Your Parent Plays Favorites

Margaret, a mother of two, was concerned about the way her parents showered attention on her daughter, eight-year-old Kate. They often invited Kate to a movie or to spend the night, but four-year-old Ben was never included in these excursions.

Often grandparents find it easier to communicate with older children. And sometimes their bond with the younger grandchild needs more time to develop.

I suggested to Margaret that she do something special with Ben when his grandparents took Kate out. She could also help the grandparents begin to establish a relationship with him by planning short activities, such as playing games like catch or I Spy or going out for ice cream.

Grandparents' favoritism can cause even more heartache when it's directed toward your sibling's children. Sometimes the solution is as simple as calling it to their attention. One mom in this situation told her mother, "You're always taking Molly's cousins to the movies, and Molly thinks you prefer them to her." Her mother was completely taken aback; she had been unaware of the effect her actions had on Molly and vowed to spend more time with her.

But it's also important that you, as an adult, accept this reality: when you're dealing with emotional issues or personality preferences, absolute equality is impossible. Many grandparents *do* have favorites. Sometimes there's a preference for one gender over the other or for a younger child rather than an older one. The other grandparents may fill the gap, or perhaps the favoritism will change over time.

For the most part, enabling your children to develop close ties with their grandparents means getting out of the way and letting the relationship develop on its own.

Playing favorites can even be hurtful to the preferred child, not just the other siblings. Anne has three kids—nine-year-old twin boys and a five-year-old girl, Suki, whom Grandma clearly favors. One day Grandma said, "Suki, you're my favorite. I love you the best." Instead of feeling happy, Suki felt guilty and upset, as though she were a traitor to her brothers.

When Your Parent Doesn't Seem to Care

Jacqui, a mother at one of my workshops, was very upset that her mother-in-law showed so little interest in her two sons, ages three and five. "What kind of grandmother is she?" she asked. "I thought grandparents were supposed to live for their grandchildren!"

When grandparents ignore your children, it can really hurt your feelings. But if you have rigid expectations of the way they're "supposed" to act, you may close off opportunities for them to become close to their grandkids on their own terms.

You may have had the fantasy that your mother or mother-in-law would spend hours with the kids, baking or reading stories. But her personality, interests, and lifestyle may not conform to your ideal. Try suggesting activities more suited to the way she is, not how you'd like her to be. Perhaps she needs a destination, such as the carousel or the public library, rather than unstructured time at your home. Keep trying, but don't take her seeming lack of interest to heart. It may be that as your children get a little older, she'll find that they have more in common with her.

It's not always possible to handle these differences with a smile and a shrug. However, you can minimize the friction if you keep your cool, your perspective, and your sense of humor.

95. Give Yourself a Break

Just because you're a parent doesn't mean you're a nonstop, twenty-four-hour-a-day nurture machine. If you don't find a way to get away—physically and emotionally—you'll have a hard time summoning the emotional resources you need for effective parenting.

Let your kids know in a very clear way that you are not always available to them at the instant they demand your attention. If your children are old enough to play on their own, they're old enough to know that there are times when you are not to be interrupted. One mother I know has made it clear that when she's in the bathroom, no one is to knock on the door or call her unless it's an emergency. Another parent who works out of her home office has a sign posted on the door: No interruptions until 4:00 P.M.

I'm sure that couples who are afraid to ever go anywhere without taking their child with them are convinced that they are dedicated parents. However, it seems to me that they're neglecting their own needs. I know parents who have never left their children with baby-sitters or taken a vacation without their kids. If you leave your children with a responsible child-care provider, most children can deal with your not being on the scene. Just because a child says, "Mommy, don't go," doesn't mean he can't cope with your leaving. In fact, when you do leave a child, it gives him the message that he can function on his own. I believe you're doing you and your child a favor by spending some time away from him. Usually parents who go away without their children come back with renewed energy and enthusiasm. Going away alone also shows your child that Mom and Dad's relationship with one another is important, too.

Many parents confuse unlimited attention with love. But sometimes it's more caring to pause and take a break for yourself. That way you'll feel less overwhelmed and resentful of your child's demands for attention. Remember, you can be a little nicer than you feel, but not a lot. And for a sleep-deprived parent—and so many are—everything becomes ten times harder. Your patience is stretched thin and your tolerance is minimal. Although your kids love you, they're not concerned about your needs. How often do you hear your children say, "Hey, Mommy, you look tired. Why don't you just lie down for a bit and we'll be extra quiet!" The best way to teach children not to be self-centered is to show them that you were not put on this earth to cater only to them.

96. Find and Keep Good Baby-Sitters

Most parents I know—especially moms—had regular baby-sitting jobs when they were preteens and teens. It was one of the few options available for earning money. "I was a great baby-sitter," one mother recalled recently. "For fifty cents an hour, I took my job very seriously. I even enjoyed being around young kids." She sighed wistfully. "I wish I could hire someone like *me* to baby-sit my kids."

Increasingly in the past twenty to thirty years, the child-care landscape has changed. Even when your child-care needs are minimal, it's hard to find good help. Teenagers, with many more options for earning money, have become scarce—and expensive. Add to that the new worries parents have about safety, and suddenly your time away from home seems loaded with land mines.

Here are a few ideas for increasing your comfort level with your baby-sitter or child-care provider:

- **When you interview the prospective caregiver, spell out your terms and expectations clearly.** You'd be surprised at how many misunderstandings there are about hours and pay. Is she handling her own transportation? What accommodations will you make if you are later than expected? Will the baby-sitter be responsible for preparing meals? Will you be leaving food for your children (and the baby-sitter) to eat?

- **Ask questions.** Find out what she would do in case of an emergency, such as a fire or a child falling down and banging his head. Find out if the person knows CPR or would be willing to take a course.

- **State your safety rules.** What should the baby-sitter do if an unfamiliar person rings the doorbell? If she sees a stranger speaking to your child on the playground? If the phone rings while she's bathing or changing the baby? Make sure you've spelled out specific guidelines for handling various situations.

- **Give the sitter a trial run.** Offer to pay him or her to spend time with your child while you're at home so that you can observe the way they interact. You can also use this as an opportunity to introduce the baby-sitter to your family rituals or teach him or her how to give the baby a bath.

- **Don't be shy about checking up on your baby-sitter.** One parent I know arranges for a friend to visit the playground when she knows her own baby-sitter will be there. The friend can observe the sitter and child together and report back. Or you might come home unannounced earlier than expected.

- **Show interest and respect.** When you come home, spend a few minutes talking with the sitter. Help her feel as if she's part of an important venture—the well-being of a child—and that you're in it together. Treat her with respect, and express your confidence and appreciation. Make sure she doesn't feel that you take her for granted.

- **Next to your phone, post information the sitter will need in an emergency.** The sample form on the next page shows basic information to include. At the top of the form, write the following information, which may seem obvious but may be necessary if the sitter gets rattled in an emergency: You are at the home of _____. The address is _____. The phone number is _____.

I still remember Phyllis, who we thought was wonderfully sweet and patient with Eric and Todd. When the boys were one and two years old, we went away for the weekend, leaving the boys with Phyllis. Upon our return our neighbors informed us that there had been a noisy party at our apartment that Saturday night. Needless to say, the guests were not invited by us! When it comes to hiring someone to watch your child, you may find to your dismay—as I did—that you're not as good a judge of character as you had thought you were.

■ **Emergency Contacts**
Where you'll be _____
Your cell phone number _____
Nearby friend _____
Nearby relative _____
Neighbor _____
Children's doctor _____
Fire department _____
Police department _____
Poison Control Center _____
Hospital _____

Another couple told me of a sitter whose visits their children looked forward to because she was so playful. One evening they returned home at 11:00 P.M. The kids were still up and greeted them at the door. The puzzled parents asked the sitter why the children were still up at that hour. She replied, "They didn't want to go to bed. They pleaded with me to let them stay up." Time to find another sitter.

A final thought: although you want your kids to bond with your caregiver, sometimes it's hard not to be jealous or feel guilty that your caregiver is there to hear your child's first word or to see him take his first step. But it's a myth that you're less important to your child than your sitter, nanny, or child-care provider. In *Child Care That Works* (Robins Lane Press, 2001), Eva and Mona Cochran reassure parents that even if they miss these precious moments, they're still number one in their child's life. They state: "Children can become emotionally attached to other people without becoming less attached to you."

97. Minimize the Pain of Divorce

One of the most stressful events in a child's life is dealing with parents who are separating or divorcing. Even when kids see their parents constantly fighting and angry with one another, many of them wish they'd stay together anyway. They're frightened and confused when faced with the inevitable changes that divorce brings. What makes this even more difficult is the fact that many children, especially younger ones, believe that somehow *they* are at fault when their parents are unable to stay together. The fact that these days divorce happens in so many families is no consolation to kids who are affected by it.

Therefore, if parents decide to separate, how can they minimize the anxiety and fear their children will experience? I believe, having worked with so many well-meaning, loving parents for so many years, that parents must never—not ever—insult the other parent in any way. I understand how difficult that can be but it's not impossible. When one parent says anything negative about the other parent in front of his or her child, that child is put in an impossible position. The child is made to suffer from guilt, divided loyalties, and fear of showing loving feelings toward the parent who is being bad-mouthed. It's fine to vent by sharing your feelings about your ex with your adult friends and any other empathic listeners, but keep those feelings from your children at all costs.

The most loving thing separated parents can do is to avoid putting children in a position where they are forced to take sides. One mother in my workshop discovered this when she tried to get her ten-year-old son to decide which parent to stay with during a holiday week. He said to her in an anguished voice, "Mom, please don't make me choose!" What's more, don't cross-examine your children about what the other parent is doing or whom he or she is seeing, no matter how curious you are or how much you want to know. It's not fair to put your kids in the no-win position of news messenger.

I admire the parent who told me that even though she thinks her ex-husband is one of the most self-centered, irresponsible people she knows, she says to her daughters: "I love my daddy, your Grandpa Bill, and I want you to love your daddy. He loves you and can't wait to see you."

An amicable divorce may sound like a contradiction in terms, but for your children, it's a necessary gift. You can divorce one another, but your kids can never divorce you. Remember, there are no ex-parents, only ex-spouses.

98. Harmonize Your Blended Family

Few blended families are like the Brady Bunch. In real life, divorce and remarriage are very stressful for kids, parents, and stepparents. For kids, divorce and remarriage mark the end of the original family as they knew it. Their fantasy that their parents might get back together is dashed when Mom or Dad takes a new partner. It's natural that kids experience divided loyalties, anger, and resentment. They also must make major readjustments—new adults, new stepsiblings, or a new home. If a move is required, it means a new school, loss of old friends, and the need to make new ones. Expect kids to be upset.

For stepparents, a blended family means being in the middle— not quite parent, not quite friend. You can't be expected to love your new stepchild instantly; you may feel frustrated or even jealous. One of the wisest experts on family relationships I know, Harriet Lerner, in her wonderful book, *The Mother Dance* (Harper Perennial, 1999), talks about the challenges facing stepmothers. When asked at the end of a talk for three pieces of advice about what stepmothers should do, she answers with her unique brand of humor: "First of all, it's very hard to be a stepmother. Second, it's *really, really* difficult. And finally, it's *much* harder than anyone could possibly anticipate at the time she decides to marry a guy who just happens to have children in a package deal."

To minimize stress and help everyone make adjustments, here are some tips:

- **Try not to create too many changes all at once.** Maintain as much continuity as possible with relatives, friends, and neighbors. Children are going through enough changes, so try to keep their old social networks in place.

- **Acknowledge the tension.** Encourage kids to express their feelings, and empathize with the difficulty of the adjustment. Sometimes they just need to vent.

- **Have family meetings to discuss problems.** Listen to each other without interrupting. Give kids opportunities to come up with their own solutions to conflicts like sharing a room with a stepsibling or dividing time between both halves of the family.

- **Keep anger toward an ex-spouse to yourself.** Settle your differences in private.

- **Let the biological parent take the leading disciplinary role.** Ideally, the stepparent should play a supportive role and defer to the biological parent in matters of discipline whenever possible. However, this is easier said than done. Especially in the case of new stepparents who have no children of their own, there are bound to be conflicts based on unrealistic expectations. Address these conflicts openly and remember that it will take time to find the right balance in your newly formed family.

- **Aim for fairly consistent rules in both households.** If curfew is 9:00 P.M. at Mom's house, it's best to have the same at Dad's. Try to reach a consensus on privileges, homework, dress, chores, and any issues that involve safety.

- **Give your stepchild time to get to know you, and expect some hostility.** Kids may initially see a stepparent as a rival for their parent's affection or an intruder who's trying to take their mother or father's place. Don't be surprised if your stepchildren don't like you, especially at first; you may not like them very much either. You love and married their parent, but you can't expect to love the children equally.

- **Don't rush into a new relationship.** Try to get to know the kids long before you make an enduring commitment to their mom or dad. See if you can anticipate and discuss problems in advance, especially if you are both bringing children to the relationship.

You'll find many more useful tips at the Stepfamily Foundation website (www.stepfamily.org), as well as at www.cyberparent .com/step, a website devoted to issues arising in second marriages with children. Keep in mind that successfully blending families can sometimes take years. It is a gradual process of getting acquainted and building trust. Stepparents can attest to the fact that it can be full of pitfalls. The first few years are the most challenging, so give it time and patience.

■ **Parent's Story: A Stepmother's Skill**

I was impressed with the skillful response of one stepmother to her teenage stepdaughter.

The stepmother told me about a recent conversation she'd had with her teenage stepdaughter, Melissa. Melissa's mother died when she was only five, and she's been living with her father and stepmother for almost a decade. Melissa and her stepmother have actually become very close, but whenever her stepmother enforces a limit that Melissa resents, Melissa becomes hostile. Last week, when the stepmother was enforcing a rule that Melissa didn't like, Melissa said, "You're not my mother, and you can't make me." The stepmother said, "That's true. I'm not your mother. But I'm the best thing you've got going for you, and I expect you to be home by midnight. That's your curfew, and it's not up for negotiation." Case closed.

99. Lighten Up

When my children were young, I saw parenting more as a job than a pleasure—and it was a job for which I felt poorly qualified. I was constantly on my guard, fearful of making a mistake that would harm my boys for life. I gave too much weight to mundane decisions—from what they ate to how they dressed to how many minutes they spent brushing their teeth to what time they had to be in bed. I failed to realize that much of their childish behavior was perfectly normal. When my sons fought, which they did frequently, I worried too much about their apparent lack of love for each other. When they refused to settle down at bedtime, I fretted about their inability to obey simple rules. If a teacher expressed even the smallest concern about either of my son's study habits, homework, or behavior, I immediately projected a grim future of failure or unemployment for them. I didn't find very much to smile about!

Today I realize how much easier life would have been for my sons and me if I had learned to lighten up. That didn't mean giving up appropriate limits or necessary rules, but not everything had to be so deadly serious. Now I can admire the mother in my workshop who, when asked how she managed to get her four children dressed and off to school on time, replied, "Easy! They go to bed with their school clothes on." Or the mother who was able to use humor to respond to the incessant whining of her three-year-old: "I'm getting so furious with you that in one more minute my eyes are going to pop out of my head and roll all the way downhill until they fall into the river!" The child began to giggle, and a crisis was averted.

Now I can appreciate the comic genius of the dad, confronted at bath time with a squirming, resistant five-year-old who *hated* having her hair washed. She fought him all the way, and when he had finally finished and her hair was all shiny and clean, she announced angrily, "Now I'm going to get mud and pour it all over my hair!" Just as he was about to reply crossly that she should stop complaining, this dad stopped himself and replied instead, "No, Annie, let's get elephant pee-pee and pour it all over your head!" In an instant, her anger turned to laughter. It was a moment of bonding. If only we parents could be less earnest, child rearing would be much more fun and rewarding.

In my workshops for parents of teens, mothers will sometimes mention how much easier it was to lighten up and see the silly side of things *before* their kids became adolescents. It's true that sometimes these ongoing, exhausting battles over rules—and almost everything else—make it much harder to pull out one of your most important survival skills: humor. I often refer parents of teens to one of my favorite books, *Get Out of My Life, but First Could You Drive Cheryl and Me to the Mall* (Noonday Press, 1992), by Anthony Wolf. The title says it all, reminding us that laughter doesn't have to disappear. And in describing the inevitability of power struggles during adolescence, Wolf writes: "To have no conflict at all is to have either a parent who does not care for a child or a child who is visiting his aunt in Florida."

100. Create Special Memories

In the last year or so, I have started to ask the same question of parents at the end of my workshops. The question is: "Can you recall something that your father or mother did with you when you were a child that made you feel really good about yourself?" Their recollections have deeply touched me. I believe the answers to this question give us all insights into what we as parents can pass on to our children *now* that will make a significant difference to both their immediate and long-term feelings about themselves. But I have also been struck by the sad fact that many parents could not recall *anything* their parents did that made them feel special, worthwhile, interesting, or a pleasure to be with.

However, what follows are some of the examples that stayed with me.

Maura related the time she was in kindergarten when she finally learned on her own how to spell her last name. (It was a very difficult Irish name like *O'Loughlin.*) She had been trying for a long time, and when she finally mastered it, she ran in to her parents, who were sitting at the dinner table, and spelled it aloud for them. She remembers how proud she felt when her parents broke into loud applause and cheers. The scene remains etched in her memory—she even described for us the color and pattern of the flowered wallpaper and the smell of the food they were eating.

One dad recalled: "My father frequently traveled on business and would sometimes take me with him on his trips, which usually entailed long bus rides. He tried to create a special ritual for each of us. I was the only one of the seven kids who went with him on the bus trips. It made me feel so important and special, having him all to myself."

Alicia was one of four daughters whose mother had to work at a full-time job. Her mother rarely was able to spend time alone with her children. Alicia told us the following story: "When I was about eight, I went to the supermarket with my mother. In the middle of one of the aisles, Mom stopped what she was doing, looked me right in the eye, and said in her most theatrical voice, 'Have you *ever* tasted a macadamia nut?' Taking a jar from the shelf, she twisted open the top and with a slow, dramatic gesture popped one right into my mouth! 'Here—these are like gold!' The moment was so unexpected and pleasurable, I never forgot it. To this day, the word *macadamia* brings back intensely happy memories for me."

Rebecca told the workshop parents of a rather unusual memory that she admitted might sound weird but recalled with pleasure: "Every so often my mom would sit on the floor with me and let me pull out her gray hairs! None of my sisters did that, only me. It was just the two of us and was such fun for me."

Roberto remembered being awakened by his father at about 4:00 A.M. several times a year on clear nights and being taken out to look at the stars and the constellations with him. Roberto now does the same thing with his son. What's more, both Roberto and his son developed a love for astronomy.

Tamika described a recurring event: "I loved shopping with my mom from the time I was very little, maybe only six years old. She'd ask for my opinion; she respected my taste, trusted my judgment, and let me have my own style. We had fun comparing prices and just schmoozing. Today (I'm in my late 30s), I call my mom and we plan special shopping days together—just the two of us."

Larry, a father in one of my workshops, shared the following memory: "When my mother and father were about to go out for the evening to a dinner party or some other dressy event, my mother would come to kiss me good night just before she left. I still remember how beautiful she looked, the smell of her perfume, and the softness of her fur coat. I loved the fact that she would linger by my bed, even though my father was waiting impatiently for her."

These are just a few of the memories mothers and fathers have shared with me. These parents are in their 20s, 30s, 40s, and 50s, from all different backgrounds and types of families.

What do these events have in common? They weren't always momentous happenings; they might even sound rather mundane to the outside world. They didn't involve spending huge amounts of money, nor were they associated with a child's receiving toys or expensive gifts. The memories were often part of a recurring event—something to look forward to or a ritual in which a child was made to feel special. Several parents commented that what made these events memorable was the feeling of being included in their parent's adult world. It made them feel very grown-up and important. Others mentioned that they felt singled out because they knew how hard it was for their mother or father to find the time to spend alone with them since they came from large families in which one or both parents worked full-time. One father said: "It was the process, not the result, that counted."

I believe that as parents we have much to learn from the previous examples. I hope they will inspire you to take the time to enjoy your kids, to discover and put into practice simple rituals and traditions that will give your children the message "I can be a source of delight and pleasure to my parents. I am fun to be with, interesting, and lovable."

A Final Word

Many years ago, I started my Parent Guidance Workshops because I watched so many parents struggle—as I myself once had—as if they were out there on their own, destined to sink or swim. We've been told countless times to just use our common sense and do what comes naturally. Common sense is usually what we learned from our own parents, who lacked parenting skills themselves. Many of us don't want to follow that same path, but we don't have a clue how to raise our kids differently. We need new models, not just what's familiar. To make child rearing even more difficult, much of the professional advice is child centered. Few resources look at things from the parents' point of view, acknowledging how often we feel exhausted, furious, guilty, or overwhelmed.

In my workshops parents feel safe expressing uncomfortable, "unacceptable" feelings. The workshops provide an environment that enables them to get past these feelings. In the informal, secure setting of these workshops, no feeling is off-limits.

One mother said to me, "I feel like a rotten mother when I admit that I'd like to bundle up my seven-year-old and send him to camp for life." Another parent—a wonderful dad whom I respect and admire for his empathy—confessed, "Yesterday, I wanted to dangle my son out of the window by his heels!"

Such feelings are completely normal and OK—as long as you don't act on them! As we've said throughout this book, wisdom isn't automatically bestowed upon us with the arrival of a baby. Even though we can all benefit from guidance, it's essential to choose your mentors and friends and decide for yourself whose advice you'll accept and whose you'll reject.

You don't have to join a parenting group to realize that you're not alone. You can get support from your local community center, from your friends, and from your children's school. There are countless resources available through books, the Internet, and parenting magazines. If you need a place to start, I invite you to visit my website, www.samalin.com, to find out how we can all join together in this fascinating task of raising the next generation. Remember, parenting is the only job for which once you're *fully* qualified, you'll be unemployed! No matter how old your children are, it's never too late.

Index

About the Author

Nancy Samalin, a pioneer in the field of parent education, is the bestselling author of three groundbreaking books, a workshop leader, and an internationally known keynote speaker.

While raising her two sons, Samalin discovered firsthand how difficult it is to be a parent. She became aware of the self-defeating patterns many of us repeat with our children despite our love and good intentions. Convinced others could benefit from the parenting skills she had acquired, she obtained her master's degree in counseling from Bank Street College and founded Parent Guidance Workshops in 1976. Parent Guidance Workshops offers parents of toddlers through teens a safe place to learn positive discipline skills and improved communication. Much of the information in Samalin's books and talks was inspired by the openness and candor of thousands of parents who have participated in these workshops over the last twenty-five years.

Her first book, *Loving Your Child Is Not Enough*, is considered to be her signature work. In this book she shows how to discipline in a firm yet loving way. Ann Pleshette Murphy, former editor of *Parents* magazine, refers to the book as "a child-rearing classic that belongs on the night table of every parent's home."

In her second book, *Love and Anger: The Parental Dilemma*, Samalin helps parents deal with their anger toward their children, surely one of the most challenging issues that all parents face. *Love and Anger* won *Child* magazine's award for the best parenting book of 1991. Adele Faber described it as "an honest look at how children can drive the most loving parent to periodic madness, along with practical suggestions for how to cope." The *Seattle Post-Intelligencer* wrote: "It is not just that Samalin has a sense of humor. What separates her from so many experts is that she has been there herself."

Loving Each One Best, Samalin's third book, is a clear and compassionate guide to raising siblings. Dr. Ron Taffel, author of *Parenting by Heart*, calls it "a wonderful book. It should be handed out as required reading when we leave the hospital with number two." A reviewer from Minnesota has this to say: "I've read many good books about siblings, but this is far and away the most practical and insightful guide I have found. Reading this book was like talking to a friend who understands."

Samalin's books have been a source of inspiration to countless parents around the world and have been translated into Spanish, French, German, Portuguese, Chinese, and Japanese.

In *Loving Without Spoiling* and in her workshops and lectures, Samalin's approach to parents continues to be both compassionate and practical, enabling them to turn their good intentions into more effective ways to bring out the best in their kids. Many parents who have studied with Samalin, heard her speak, or attended her workshops talk about the profound impact she has had on their lives.

She has been an immensely popular speaker throughout the United States and abroad for many years. For more than two decades she has been giving inspiring presentations to parents and professionals at corporations, public and independent schools, universities, hospitals, community centers, and various parenting programs. She specializes in a hands-on approach that gives parents practical tools they can put into immediate use. Samalin has an upbeat and entertaining speaking style that places her in great demand as a speaker both nationally and internationally. She is a gifted presenter whose warmth and empathy for parents and the daily challenges they face is honestly conveyed in her keynotes. People often approach her after her talks and say, "It sounds like you've been living in my house!"

For Further Information

The author welcomes your personal feedback, any anecdotes you might have, and what strategies worked for you that you believe would be helpful for other parents. Please contact Nancy Samalin with this information by E-mailing her at **nancysamalin@ aol.com**.

By visiting Samalin's website (**www.samalin.com**), you may:

- schedule a keynote speech or workshop
- subscribe to her online newsletter
- find out about her speaking schedule